Seeking Sanctuary

Seeking Sanctuary

A History of Refugees in Britain

Jane Marchese Robinson

PEN & SWORD
HISTORY

First published in Great Britain in 2020 by
Pen & Sword History
An imprint of
Pen & Sword Books Ltd
Yorkshire – Philadelphia

ISBN 978 1 52673 961 2

Typeset by Mac Style
Printed and bound by CPI Group (UK) Ltd, Croydon, CR0 4YY

Pen & Sword Books Limited incorporates the imprints of Atlas,
Archaeology, Aviation, Discovery, Family History, Fiction, History,
Maritime, Military, Military Classics, Politics, Select, Transport,
True Crime, Air World, Frontline Publishing, Leo Cooper, Remember
When, Seaforth Publishing, The Praetorian Press, Wharncliffe
Local History, Wharncliffe Transport, Wharncliffe True Crime
and White Owl.

For a complete list of Pen & Sword titles please contact

PEN & SWORD BOOKS LIMITED
47 Church Street, Barnsley, South Yorkshire, S70 2AS, England
E-mail: enquiries@pen-and-sword.co.uk
Website: www.pen-and-sword.co.uk

Or

PEN AND SWORD BOOKS
1950 Lawrence Rd, Havertown, PA 19083, USA
E-mail: Uspen-and-sword@casematepublishers.com
Website: www.penandswordbooks.com

Contents

Acknowledgements

I would like to thank the following:
My husband, Tony Marchese for his advice and enduring support.
Marie Cappart, Family Historian who traced my grandmother, Jeanne Marie Krott in the Brussels Archives
Dr Jameson Tucker of Plymouth University who pointed me to a variety of useful Huguenot Sources
Gaynor Haliday for her painstaking editing.
People have been generous in their contributions to this book and I am particularly grateful to the following for their personal accounts:
Ildiko McIndoe formerly Homolya
Bill Meswania
Julia Meiklejohn
Baki Ejupi
Celia Edwards
And many thanks to Cathy Murphy and Andy Varley for accommodating and feeding me when I visited the archives.

5 August 2020

Introduction

Throughout the ages, people have fled their homeland, nation or country of origin in the face of danger and threats to themselves and their families. War and persecution are powerful motivators, impelling people to seek safety and sanctuary. Some will seek a safe place in their own land, others will cross a border into a neighbouring country, yet others will undertake a potentially dangerous sea crossing. It follows that people seeking sanctuary in Britain would have had to make that journey by sea over the many centuries.

The term refugee was enshrined in the 'Convention and Protocol relating to the Status of Refugees',[1] published by the United Nations High Commission for Refugees (UNHCR) in 1951. It is sometimes referred to simply as the '1951 Convention'. It was written following the United Nations Declaration of Human Rights in 1948, itself developed in the wake of the Second World War which witnessed the greatest movement of peoples in world history. Article 14 of that declaration recognised the right of persons to seek asylum from persecution in other countries and it is the centrepiece of international refugee protection today. The Convention of 1951 sought to protect the rights of all citizens and ensure their freedoms from many oppressions. It provided the word 'refugee' with a legal definition: 'someone who is outside his or her own country and unable to be protected by that country owing to a well-founded fear of being persecuted for reasons of race, religion, nationality, membership of a particular social group or political opinion'. The Convention was agreed internationally following the genocide of so many Jewish people and other refugees who sought, both successfully and unsuccessfully, to escape the Nazi regime.

Entering into force on 22 April 1954, the Convention defined how refugees should be helped and was intended to ensure that people would not be blocked or prevented from seeking sanctuary away from persecution in their homeland. Ratified by 145 nations, it outlines the rights of the displaced as well as the legal obligations of the states to protect them. The core principle is 'non-refoulement' which means a refugee must not be returned to a country where he or she could face serious threats to life or freedom. This is considered a customary rule of international law.

However, the term refugee has been used since the seventeenth century and originally referred to the Huguenots who came from France. Indeed, the word derives from the French word *refugier*, a verb meaning to seek shelter or to protect. These were Protestant people who fled from France when the Edict of Nantes, which had granted them religious liberty and civil rights, was revoked in 1685. Around 400,000 Huguenots fled in the ensuing years. It is estimated that 40–50,000 sought refuge in England, most arriving by boat.

However, within a decade the term was in general use in England to describe anyone fleeing religious or political persecution.

People began to seek sanctuary in this country from the sixteenth century onwards as the result of religious persecution of Protestant minorities in the Spanish Netherlands, which roughly equates to modern Belgium. Moslems and Jews expelled by Spain in 1495 were mainly given sanctuary in other European countries and Turkey. However, a small number of Jewish converts, known as 'conversos', may have reached London under another guise. These people would practise their religion secretly and maintained links with a trading group of Jewish people in Amsterdam.

This book seeks to provide an introduction to the history of those seeking refuge in this country and to recount, wherever possible, the stories of those who sought sanctuary here; why they fled, how they travelled and how they were received in this country.

It is important, however, to state from the outset that the terms 'refugee' and 'migrant', though sometimes used interchangeably and often confused, are not the same. People migrate in search of a better life than they can find in their place of birth or country of origin. This may be due to famine or poverty or because they are attracted to another country where they envisage they have the prospects of improved economic outcomes. Sometimes they are recruited to work in another country. There is no implied criticism of such aspirations. The origins of the human species provide evidence that people have moved location, whether by 'push or pull' reasons, since the dawn of time.

However, refugees are people who are compelled to seek sanctuary away from their homeland owing to persecution, torture and in fear of their lives. It is important to make this distinction, since both in the modern media and at times in the past the myth has been propagated that refugees have arrived in this country purely for their own pecuniary advantage. Nowadays it has been suggested that 'they are just here to claim benefits' or alternatively to take work from the indigenous British people. Thus, refugees can become scapegoats and this view has been promoted by elements of the media either through ignorance or design.

As a child of parents who lived through the Second World War, the author was aware of the atrocities meted out by the Nazis. As time progressed, the author learnt about the barriers to those refugees seeking sanctuary which resulted in unnecessary deaths. However, the first experience of refugees was seeing the Ugandan Asian people expelled by Idi Amin as they walked down the steps of an aircraft at Heathrow Airport, shivering in the English winter of 1972. Many other groups followed over the ensuing years and were greeted with varying levels of welcome. These peoples and indeed those who had arrived before them are the subject of this book.

The commencement of a personal journey occurred later. In 2006, two years after the death of the author's mother, she discovered an autograph book that had belonged to her grandmother in the years after 1919, whilst working at the Strand Palace Hotel in London. The author had always known that her grandmother was Belgian but beyond that her mother had told her very little. Unfortunately, her grandmother had died before the author was born. The autograph book provided a real insight into life in a central London hotel just after the end of the Great War. Guests from Canada, Egypt and France had annotated the autograph book and some had taken the trouble to draw a cartoon or a small watercolour. Suddenly the author's grandmother became a real person and she wanted to know more about her and how she came to be living and working in London. Research on the internet lead her immediately to the astonishing story.

She discovered that 250,000 Belgians had fled to Britain when the German tanks rolled across their homeland and that they had been welcomed throughout the UK.

The author attempted to trace her grandmother's origins in both the National and Metropolitan Archives but without success. It was to be another eleven years before the author discovered the papers relating to Jeanne Marie Krott, after the historian, Simon Fowler, recommended contact with a Ms Marie Cappart, a fantastic family historian in Belgium. The records being sought for such a long time were the official records of Belgians seeking sanctuary in England and though thought to have been lost or destroyed they were in fact filed in the National Archives in Brussels. It was a wonderful find. But, in the meantime, the author had discovered copious information concerning other Belgian refugees who had come to Britain in 1914.

This discovery and subsequent research arose when the author was learning about and seeking to help refugees first-hand, having been appointed manager at Refugee Action in Plymouth in 2003. This organisation worked with asylum seekers and refugees who had been sent to Plymouth under the government's National Asylum Seeking Service (NASS) scheme. They included Iraqis, Iranians, Eritreans, Somalis, Zimbabweans and Sudanese.

Later, when the author was able to assimilate these many stories and to see her grandma's life in context, she knew that she wanted to write about those many people over the centuries who had sought sanctuary here in Britain. The author is therefore grateful to the publishers Pen and Sword for providing her with this opportunity. She is, of course, solely responsible for the content of this book.

Chapter 1

The First Protestant Refugees

In the late medieval times (in the fourteenth and fifteenth centuries), there had been growing discontent about the power and wealth of the Catholics, as well as particular doctrinal issues throughout Europe. People began to question the power of the bishop and corruption in the church. To obtain a place in heaven people were supposed to perform good deeds but Catholic churches were enriching themselves selling indulgences which obviated the need to do anything.

The leading critic was a German, Martin Luther, who, in 1517, nailed his 'Ninety-five theses' (or Disputation on the Power of Indulgences) on the door of the church at Wittenberg, a town on the River Elbe in eastern Germany. He was not alone, since from the 1530s John Calvin was also challenging the foundations of the established Roman Catholic Church from his newly established base in Geneva. From here, the Bible was translated into French and was disseminated across France. Their writings, teachings and sermons were to spearhead a movement that would lead to the biggest schism in European history.

It is no exaggeration to say that for the people of the sixteenth century, religion was at the core of their existence. It determined how they worshipped and it permeated their daily lives. Marriage, birth and death rituals, the punishment of wrongdoers and crop planting and harvesting were all dictated by religion.

In the Catholic religion, the priest was all powerful and in a world where few could read, his interpretation of the Bible would be unquestioned.

This gave him unrivalled influence over his flock, with the possibility of petty corruption by means of selling indulgences or pardons or taking sexual liberties with young women in his flock. At a higher level in the church hierarchy, bishops and prelates kept mistresses.

The new religion, later to become known as Protestantism, was popular because it questioned these accepted norms and strove to find a purer, unsullied way of living, based more literally on the teachings of the Bible.

It took hold particularly in Germany, parts of France and the Spanish Netherlands, the latter of which was equivalent to modern Belgium.

The Spanish Netherlands were ruled from Madrid by Phillip II of Spain. As a Catholic monarch, he wished to stamp out any Protestant heresies. Therefore, seeking to impose his authority, by stamping down on any unrest, he sent the Duke of Alva to the Spanish Netherlands in June 1568 to suppress the Protestants in this Spanish colony. There were two counts (Egmond and Hoorne) who, although Catholic, seemed to Alva to lend their support to the local Protestant people, which infuriated him.[1] He first imprisoned them for a year and he then had them beheaded in the main square in Brussels. This act ignited fury and the people rose up in protest. However, with 10,000 troops, many of them mercenaries, Alva had the rebellion put down mercilessly. In the northern Dutch-speaking region many people fled to the Netherlands, and in the south many Walloon- and French-speaking peoples fled to Britain. Pieter Bruegel's famous painting *Massacre of the Innocents* ostensibly showed the biblical Herod's massacre of male babies after Jesus's birth. However, in the painting, all the soldiers are dressed in Spanish uniforms which suggests that Bruegel was making reference to, and commenting on, such atrocities.

In 1568, after a great influx of Protestants fled from the Spanish Netherlands to England, the Duchess of Parma, who was acting as regent in the Spanish Netherlands, told her brother Philip II that in a few days around 100,000 people had fled to England with their money and goods. She advised him that they could only enrich England and impoverish the Netherlands.

These people settled in a number of towns including Canterbury, Norwich, Sandwich, Southampton, Colchester and Maidstone, and of course London. These people followed such skilled occupations as silk weavers, dyers, woollen and linen weavers. In the sixteenth century, there was no such term as refugee; by people in England these newcomers were dubbed 'Strangers'.

Elizabeth I, a Protestant and the reigning English monarch, was welcoming of these people not only because she essentially shared their religious beliefs but also because these Strangers offered many advanced skills and thus were of immense economic value to the country. Reflecting the religious divide, the Pope on the other hand described them as 'terrible people' and condemned Elizabeth for taking them in.

You will find that often all sixteenth and seventeenth century Protestant exiles who came to Britain are called 'Huguenots' and it is the view that the Huguenot Society favour. But where you see the term 'Stranger' or 'Walloon' they will be talking about those people of the sixteenth century who fled from the Spanish Netherlands.[2]

Just as the 'Strangers and Walloons' were settling into their new life in England, a most terrible event took place in France. Ongoing and bitter warfare had been taking place between the different religions. This led to two days, in August 1572, when a massacre of Protestants took place.[3]

Leading Huguenots were present in Paris in order to attend the wedding of the Protestant, Henri of Navarre, who was later to become Henri IV of France. At that festive gathering, an attempted assassination of Gaspard de Coligny, the military and political leader of the Huguenots, occurred, which triggered the massacre. Ostensibly it was ordered by King Charles IX but it is widely believed to have been instigated by his mother, Catherine de Medici. Starting in Paris, it spread to other major towns namely Bordeaux, Toulouse, Lyons, Bourges, Rouen, Orleans, Mieux, Angers, La Charite, Saumar, Gaillac and Troyes.

Some 3,000 people were slaughtered in one night in Paris. Estimated numbers elsewhere were very high. It became known as the St Bartholomew's Day Massacre, named after the saint's day on which it fell, which was 24 August. It was perceived within the Catholic hierarchy to be a righteous killing and Pope Gregory arranged for a medal to be struck in celebration! With art reflecting its terrible realities, Christopher Marlowe wrote a play called the Massacre of Paris, which was published in 1593.

Unsurprisingly, Phillip II also gave his approval. Again, many Protestants fled to England, fearful of the consequences of following their own religion, in the knowledge that others had gone before them and that Queen Elizabeth would welcome them. They followed the earlier Strangers who had settled in the east and south of the country in such places as Rye, Norwich, Sandwich and Canterbury. These latest exiles particularly favoured Canterbury. The generous welcome to these newcomers provided by the English monarchy was not always reflected by working people here. The Strangers were industrious people who brought their own skills and this potential competition worried many ordinary workers in England. In 1576, the cordwainers, the Elizabethan word for shoemakers, complained about the Strangers to the queen.[4]

They wanted to know if they were 'denizens' which meant they would have rights to stay in the country. If that was the case, the cordwainers knew that they would continue to be in competition with these foreign incomers.

If the incomers ended up being 'naturalised' they would have full rights of citizenship. Ten years later the London apprentices, a powerful group, raised an insurgence against foreigners in the city. Following that, in 1592, the retailers complained that these newcomers could sell their goods in areas that were forbidden to their own people.

This latter outcome was an anomaly resulting from a law made in the time of Queen Mary. These complaints came from English workers who felt their livelihood under threat. But, fortunately for the Protestant strangers, this did not come from those in power, who could have encouraged a more hostile response if they had wished. Nowadays some of those in power may encourage prejudice against refugees as a way of creating scapegoats to further their own ends.

It wasn't just the workers who had major objections to the Strangers. In 1570, a group of Norfolk gentlemen from the south of the county plotted to attack the strangers at Harleston fair and evict them from their land. Their plot was uncovered and Queen Elizabeth herself pursued a charge of High Treason against them. She clearly meant business, as three of the men were hung, drawn and quartered as a lesson to others! She enjoined her citizens to leave the Strangers in peace to pursue their work. That work was extremely profitable and provided a significant income for the Crown and it is to be noted that after Elizabeth's death, in 1621, the Lord Keeper (John Williams, Bishop of Lincoln) praised the wealth that the Strangers had brought. And so it was that the Protestant Strangers lived a quiet industrious life, grateful to be able to practise their religion in peace.

Another indication of how supportive Elizabeth I was to these Strangers is how she gave the Protestants at Canterbury the cathedral's undercroft to use for their worship in perpetuity. This was a great tribute.

These many positive attributes may explain why in 1598, when a new king, Henri IV, came to power in France, his Edict of Nantes, aimed at ameliorating the environment for Protestants and Huguenots, did not entice so many French people to return home. Interestingly Henri IV was the same Henri of Navarre whose wedding was the backdrop to the St Bartholomew's Day massacre in 1572. His edict now allowed Protestants to worship freely in France as long as they did not attempt to proselytise or preach their religion to others. But for people settled in Britain with their trade protected and with the possibility that their children might wish to stay and marry there was little to draw them back. It was the revoking of this edict in 1685 that sent another group of French Protestants to flee in their thousands.

The number of Strangers was largely stable but increased from time to time with further persecution in Europe. In Canterbury in 1634, there were 900 which by 1665 had risen to 1,300. Of those, 126 were master weavers and they employed 759 English people, an indication that the community was settled and bedded in. In 1676, the king, Charles II, presented the Protestants/Strangers with a charter and they became a company. All the signs were of respectability.

Where they had settled they were usually made welcome by employers and masters since it was believed they enhanced local prosperity. In Glastonbury, Somerset, far from the eastern counties, the Duke of Somerset granted them lands, money to buy wool and the right to employ local people.

It is interesting that this is not the first record of the Strangers employing local people.

Soon after the Strangers' arrival, London developed as their centre, since being the capital city it naturally drew in newcomers.[5] It was the seat of the Royal court and of Parliament. It hosted law courts and was a major port with international links. It was also the administrative capital and seat of the monarch, meaning that it could provide support either directly or by encouraging other bodies to raise monies for these newcomers. London was also the centre of fashion, theatre and cultured eating places.

The Strangers were in fact taxed twice (such were the peculiarities of medieval tax law), which made them a profitable proposition. Between

1566 and 1569, a list was made of all Strangers in London. Such a 'census' would enable subsequent taxation to be carried out efficiently. This was done by requiring every ward to send a list of Strangers and their occupations, how long they had been in residence there, and what church they attended.

London had two major Protestant churches. Edward VI, the boy king and son of Henry VIII, had given the Strangers a church at Austin Friars, in the present-day City of London, in 1550. Those members of the congregation were of Dutch origin. The other church, in Threadneedle Street, was for French-speaking Strangers. Both tended to attract newcomers by language and by their religious practice and to a large extent the distinction between them dictated how the two communities developed. Thus it was that in the east of London, and primarily in Spitalfields, the artisan Strangers developed the weaving industry.

In the west of London, Soho, a slightly higher class of refugees came to settle: soldiers, particularly officers, intellectuals and tradesmen involved in fashionable trades such as hairdressing, jewellery, silversmithing, tailoring, watchmaking, wig making and the like. New arrivals would be drawn to a trade they were already familiar with and which would determine where they settled.

Robin Gwynne, in his book *The Huguenots of London* (reprinted 2018), cites figures for the occupations of Protestants in the seventeenth century, based on research undertaken by E.H. Varley in 1939:[5]

	Eastern London	Western London
Doctors and Ministers	160	86
Food, drink and clothing	24	207
Jewellers, Clockmakers etc.	8	119
Merchants	31	100
Military	4	131
Naval	60	11
Perruquiers	8	53
Textile workers	465	44
All others	81	330

NB: A *perruquier* is someone who makes and sells hairpieces.

Rye was another place where the Strangers came to live, not surprisingly as it was on the coast facing northern France across a narrow stretch of the Channel.

Captain Sore, who transported people across the Channel, kept records and may have liaised with the queen. From 1562, the town of Rye willingly gave shelter to large numbers of Protestant refugees fleeing from persecution in France and in 1582, of a total population of around 3,500, there were over 1,500 people of French extraction living in the town. For a while they had their own ministers and held their own services in the church but by the end of the century, they were attending ordinary services.

Norwich

Norwich was the centre of a large textile industry, but in the sixteenth century this industry was struggling to compete economically because there had been a decline in skills.[6] The city was also recovering from destruction of the Kett Rebellion almost twenty years before. The city needed to employ more workers and these were found from those Strangers from the Spanish Netherlands in the 1560s who were fleeing the rampages of the Duke of Alva. They were as welcome in Norwich as their counterparts were in London. The Strangers taught local workers how to produce new types of cloth using different methods, which provided a significant boost to the textile industry and the local economy. They also helped to rebuild the whole area north of the River Wensum after it had been devastated by a freak fire in 1507. They supported English parishes by donating money to them, and Dutch and French schools were established in the area.

Norwich City Football Club is known as 'The Canaries'. The name's origin derives from the Strangers. In their high-ceilinged rooms, where they spent many hours weaving, they kept the canaries for company and for the enjoyment of their melodic song. The Strangers were famous for their skills in breeding canaries, and the football club's name is one of their most famous legacies. Many people who live in Norwich now are descendants of these Strangers, whose influence can still be seen in buildings around the region, as well as in the Norfolk diction. The Strangers' Hall Museum in Norwich provides a wealth of information relating to these people.

Canterbury

The Huguenot settlement in Canterbury began after the authorities considered the community in Sandwich, Kent, to have grown too large.[6] A hundred families were accepted in 1575. Its numbers continued to swell in the years following the St Bartholomew's Massacre in France, and a second revolt in the Netherlands, and it came to represent the largest foreign population outside of London. The welcome that was extended to the refugees in Kent was in many ways similar to that in Norwich. Again, this in large part reflected the perceived benefit to the local economy, particularly the potential for developing the textile industry. Using the textile processing and weaving techniques learnt on the continent, new draperies were established here and in other textile towns. Rather than making traditional woollen fabrics, they produced lighter fabrics, made from a mix of fibres, suitable for export to Europe. The benefits led the Privy Council to protect these Stranger weavers in Canterbury when they were attacked by local people. And many successful Spitalfields' weavers established the viability of their businesses in Canterbury.

The Huguenot congregation in Canterbury was first allowed to worship at St Alphege Church, but as their numbers grew, and as mentioned previously, they were invited to use the undercroft of the cathedral. Later the Strangers were given permission to use the Black Prince Chantry in the western crypt and when in occupation, between 1576 and 1895, members of the congregation painted the arches with cartouches containing biblical quotations.

Fragments can still be made out today through the whitewash in places, but in the chapel, above the crypt door is the only complete relic of those days, when the chapel served as an entrance lobby. This French Walloon Church, as it later became known, is where the *Eglise Protestante Française de Cantorbéry* (The French Protestant Church of Canterbury) still meets today, a lasting legacy of the Strangers' arrival to this country and this period of history.

Chapter 2

The Huguenots and the Revocation of the Edict of Nantes

After the terrifying massacres of French Protestants following St Bartholomew's Day 1585, the new king, Henri IV, issued the Edict of Nantes which offered a degree of tolerance to Protestants in France. It meant that they could follow their religion quietly as long as they did not try to convert others. It was hoped that some who had fled to England might return but as noted in an earlier chapter this was not very successful. Many were settled in England and did not want to risk an uncertain life at home. Then in 1610, Henri himself was assassinated by a prominent Catholic. Henri IV, previously Henri of Navarre and dubbed the 'good king', had been considered a tolerant and helpful king but his successor Louis XIII did not follow his example.

Toleration diminished and once Louis XIV succeeded his father in 1643, persecution had begun in earnest. Decrees were issued against Huguenots, churches were destroyed and lithographs from the time show children being flung out of windows to force their parents to convert.

From 1681, the Dragoons, armed cavalry officers, were unleashed on Huguenot households. They were billeted, fed and watered at the family's expense and cruel behaviour was encouraged against the inhabitants, designed to force people to convert. The dragonnades were much feared; it was said that if a town's people saw their approach they would seek to convert immediately. Then on the 22 October 1685, Louis revoked the Edict of Nantes which had been enacted by Henri IV and simultaneously enacted the Edict of Fontainebleau. This latter edict ensured that any who opted to leave lost their citizenship and were thus barred from returning. But fear of ongoing and sustained persecution still impelled thousands to leave.

It is worth noting at this point where the term 'Huguenot' might come from.[1] From the literature it is evident that nobody is exactly sure of the origin of the word 'Huguenot'. One thing is agreed upon, however, and that is when it was first used, the term was one of derision used against those who rejected Catholicism and chose to follow a new 'reformed' religion in Europe.

One suggestion is that it may be derived from the French word *Huguon* – meaning 'One who walks by night'; this being a reference to the fact that Huguenots were forced to meet in secret at night to avoid detection.

It may also be a combination of Flemish and German words. In the Flemish corner of France, Bible students who gathered in each other's houses to study secretly were called *Huis Genooten*, meaning 'House mates'. Another suggestion is that it was derived from the German word *Eidgenossen*, which means 'confederate'. Others believe that the word was derived from the name Hugues. Hugues was a religious leader and politician in Geneva, who was a strong follower of Calvin's teachings. He led a group called the 'Confederate Party', so-called because it favoured an alliance between the City-State of Geneva and the Swiss Confederation.

Not all Huguenots came to England. As an enterprising group they sought sanctuary in various European countries and beyond; thus, they went to Prussia, Sweden and Holland. They also travelled to South Africa and Canada. It was the Huguenots in South Africa who started wine production, harnessing the local climate and using skills acquired in France.

Like their Walloon and Stranger brothers before them, it was necessary for the fleeing Huguenots to take to the sea to arrive in England. Like many asylum-seekers taking to boats in the Mediterranean today, their journeys could be perilous. Two boys who became successful in adult life made a perilous journey by boat from Bordeaux to Southampton, hidden in wine barrels. This would have taken them across the unstable waters of the Bay of Biscay and must have been a terrifying experience for the young boys.

Those arriving after 1688 were lucky to arrive in a country with a fiercely Protestant monarchy. William of Orange in the Netherlands had secured the British throne together with his queen and cousin, Mary. They ascended to the throne as part of the Glorious Revolution, the coming together of the monarchies of England and Holland. William was from the province of Orange. The Walloon Strangers, who had arrived in this country previously, received support and largesse from Queen Elizabeth. These Protestant refugees, now commonly called Huguenots, who came after the Revocation of the Edict of Nantes were awarded the same level of support from the new monarchy.

From 1697 onwards in the reign of William and Mary these refugees were given monies from the Royal Purse on a regular basis. The beautiful hand-inscribed ledger detailing payments to different towns and cities is shown in the plate section and is headed: 'To the Poor French Refugees in Several Counties of England'.[2]

Canterbury	£180
Exeter	£22 10s
Plymouth	£45
Stonehouse	£28 16s
Dover	£12
La Rye	£27

The destination of the last donation of £27 (La Rye) is most likely to be Rye on the south coast, where even as early as 1582 there were over 1,500 people of French extraction living in the town, out of a total population of around 3,500.

It is estimated that about 50,000 Huguenots came here at that time and a further 10,000 went to Ireland, then a colony of Britain. Many settled in London but they also made their homes in places such as Bristol and Southampton. The West Country was a popular destination with populations in Exeter, Plymouth, Bideford and Barnstaple. These would likely be the destinations for boats from the west of France from such towns as Bordeaux and La Rochelle, which were fiercely Protestant.

Barnstaple

The first Huguenot refugees in Barnstaple arrived in 1685; the year the Edict of Nantes was revoked.[3] The way in which the town responded to the new arrivals is recorded in the diary of Jacques Fontaine, born in Jenouille (or Genouillé), France in 1658. He describes the welcome he received from Protestant hosts:

After paying for our passage, I had only twenty gold pistoles left, but God had not conducted us in safety to a haven there to leave us to perish with hunger; the good people of Barnstaple had compassion upon us, took us into their houses, and treated us with the greatest kindness; thus God raised up for us fathers and mothers, and brothers and sisters, in a strange land.

To support the Huguenots living in the town, Barnstaple received funds from the Civil List during William and Mary's reign. And shortly after their arrival, the local authorities gave them St Anne's Chapel (now a museum and community centre) as a place of worship; services were held there in French until 1762. Fontaine stayed with a local merchant, called Downe, and was joined in Barnstaple by further Huguenot migrants. In 1838, his diary was translated and published under the title *A Tale of the Huguenots or Memoirs of a French Refugee Family*. He records his business failures and successes and trials in love and later marriage.

The Huguenot influence on Barnstaple, as in many of the towns in which the refugees settled, was ongoing, owing to their introduction of different divisions of wool manufacture and dyeing processes, for which the town became famous. Jean Ulrich Passavant, a Huguenot from Strasbourg, created a table carpet depicting Barnstaple's coat of arms and presented it to the town. The carpet also displayed the name of the mayor, Monier Roch Esq, and the date, 1761. The Roch family, which was of Huguenot descent, was prominent in Barnstaple. Both Matthew Roch and his son Monier established themselves within the local community and served several times as the town's mayor. In 1791, Monier Roch founded the Barnstaple Bank and was borough treasurer. A portrait of Matthew Roch can be seen in Barnstaple's Guildhall.

Bideford

Sitting astride the River Torridge, near to the estuary, Bideford has been a strategic port for many years, dealing in shipbuilding and repairs. Increasingly it became a port for trade and for people leaving Devon and its hinterland to cross the Atlantic. In the other direction came the Protestant refugees fleeing France.

Running off from Allhalland Street is the cul-de-sac of Chapel Lane, named after the Huguenot Chapel that used to be at the far end of the lane. A French Huguenot congregation was set up in Bideford in 1695 and this lane lead to their church. Refugees were well settled by then.

Plymouth

C.W. Bracken, in his paper for the Devonshire association (1934), describes the arrival of an overcrowded boat at Plymouth and is told of another bound for Dartmouth.[4] On 6 September 1681, he quotes from a local paper: 'a little French fishing smack which was open and crowded with forty or fifty Protestants from La Rochelle landed'.

They were told that in all four boats had left and one had landed at Dartmouth, although Plymouth was the intended destination. Sadly, it was not known what happened to the other two boats. Thus, even before the Revocation, fear of the dragonnades was driving people to the desperate measure of boarding a small boat to set sail across the Bay of Biscay and through the widest part of the English Channel.

Many Huguenots decided to flee to Plymouth. This was almost certainly due to existing trading connections between Huguenot families and the port of Plymouth and the 1680s saw successive boatloads fleeing persecution and seeking sanctuary in the town. A large Huguenot community settled in Plymouth with another at Stonehouse, then a separate town to the west. These entrepreneurial and highly skilled merchants and traders found themselves at ease in their new surroundings and provided new opportunities and contacts to the traders and merchants of their new home. French language services were held at St George's Chapel and at the old friary on Southside Street as the Protestants sought to continue their faith in their mother tongue.

The Plymouth Huguenots were non-conformist. They followed a Calvinist liturgy because they could not worship alongside Anglicans.

They were lucky to have high-ranking support locally. The local gentry, the Edgcumbes, helped them obtain a licence for a vicar and later gave them support when the curate at East Stonehouse had refused to allow Huguenot interments. They also had support from a Reverend John Quick, who in 1662 had been ejected from his living in Brixton, a village close to Plymouth.

A large Huguenot meeting place in Southside Street, in Plymouth's Barbican is now the site of the famous Plymouth Gin Distillery!

Another early Huguenot meeting place in How Lane, also in the Barbican, suffered a dwindling population coupled with a deteriorating building. The virtual collapse of the balcony forced the community to move. By the early eighteenth century, the congregation had moved to a church in Stonehouse.

Mr Bracken also mentions an entry, in 1790, in the Stonehouse church records which shows the baptism of a Georges Marie Bertrand from Lower Brittany whose parents were fleeing the French Revolution. Given the cruelties meted out in Brittany by French Revolutionary zealots, which are described in Chapter 4, it is unsurprising that a family would flee Brittany and cross the channel.

Exeter

Outside of London, the largest foreign communities in England in the late seventeenth century were settled in Devon, Canterbury and East Anglia, where they made up approximately one-third of the population.[5]

In Devon itself, the largest groups were resident in Exeter and Plymouth. These settlements came about because of each town's proximity to the sea and relationship with the textile trade, where newcomers could hope to obtain work.

In Exeter there would have been opportunities for skilled weavers in the flourishing serge business. The city briefly became famous for carpet production thanks to Swiss Huguenot Claude Passavant, who purchased a London workshop in 1755, and brought many of the weavers to Exeter. The designs they wove are thought to have been bought from France. Just three Passavant carpets have survived which are now housed at the Victoria and Albert Museum, Petworth House, and the third in a private collection.

A Huguenot conformist congregation was started at St Olave's Church, on Fore Street in Exeter, in 1686. This was one of two churches used by the settlers in the city. There was also a non-conformist congregation, founded earlier in 1620. Those that attended at St Olave's were recorded to be 120 strong in 1715, under the minister Andrew Majendie. Services were conducted in French, and the church was popularly known as the French church. This ceased in 1758, when its members joined the Anglican church.

A link to Exeter's Huguenot past exists today in the gentlemen's outfitters Luget, located in the Cathedral Yard. The Lugets – Anne and James – are thought to have been French Huguenots, who married in Exeter in 1806. Their son Follet Luget, born on 17 December 1817, became a tailor and established the name's association with tailoring in the city.

Bristol

Bristol was one of a second group of towns in which new Huguenot settlements developed. From the end of the seventeenth century, between 400 and 500 Huguenots moved to Bristol, making up 2.5 per cent of the population. They received money from the Civil List, allocated by William and Mary, between 1689 and 1693.

St Mark's Church on the north-east side of College Green in Bristol was given to the Huguenots to worship by the city corporation. They used the church between 1687 and 1722, and Madame Gautier, wife of Reverend Gautier the French pastor, opened a boarding and day school.

A few of the Huguenots who settled in Bristol, came from wealthy merchant families, from La Rochelle and other French Atlantic ports, including the Peloquins, Laroche and Goizin families.

Their trading contacts in America with other Huguenot and Dutch merchants ensured they quickly established themselves in the Atlantic economy and contributed substantially to the city's prosperity.

One famous Bristol Huguenot was Francis Billo, a metalworker, who became well known for his chandeliers made in the West County. He created a ceremonial crown (circa 1733) in copper, to wear for the Processions of the Trades. It was modelled on a Royal crown and is now in the collection of Bristol Museums. Another renowned Bristol Huguenot was silversmith Solomon Egare who lived in the city before settling in America.

Dover

Dover's coastal position and proximity to France made it a natural landing and first point of settlement for Huguenot refugees. Many stayed temporarily, moving on to larger communities in London and Canterbury, or before returning home during periods of relative safety. We have seen in Chapter 1 that it was first settled by the Strangers from the Spanish Netherlands in the 1560s, followed by those fleeing the violence of the St Bartholomew's Day Massacre. Early in the seventeenth century, a census was taken of the foreign persons residing in Dover; it was found that there were seventy-seven people:

> Two were preachers of God's Word; three were physicians and surgeons; two were advocates; two esquires; three were merchants; two were schoolmasters; thirteen were drapers, butchers and other trades; twelve were mariners; eight weavers and woolcombers; twenty-five were widows and makers of bone; two were maidens; one the wife of a shepherd; one a gardener and one a non-descript male.

As in many towns where Huguenots had settled, the Dover textile industry grew and was an important means for the newcomers to earn a living. Dover, and nearby Sandwich, were particularly known for wool combing; the process of arranging the fibres so they are parallel, ready for spinning.

There was a French Church in Dover from the 1640s, following the tradition of the Flemish congregation that had been in the town since the sixteenth century. It was part of a triumvirate of churches with Guisnes, in northern France, and Cadzand, in the Dutch province of Zeeland, which had a mobile population, many of whom moved to Dover and then back onto the mainland. The Dover Huguenot settlement was considered sizable enough between 1689 and 1693 to receive monies from the Civil List given by William and Mary.

Rye

In 1685, a further fifty Huguenot families arrived after the Revocation of the Edict of Nantes and joined the earlier Strangers who had settled there. Some of the Huguenots' descendants worship in the church to this day. The clock of the church was made in about 1561–2 by the Huguenot, Lewys Billiard, who was paid £30 for his work. It is one of the oldest turret clocks in the country which is still functioning.

'Jeake's House' in Rye originally belonged to the Jeake family. Of Huguenot origin, the family's first settler in Rye appears to have been a late sixteenth-century merchant, William Jeaque (a possible corruption of Jacques). His son Henri set up a bakery in the High Street. William's grandson, Samuel Jeake junior, made his living as a wool merchant and Jeake House was previously a storehouse for his wool. Today, Jeake's House is a hotel.

Southampton

In one corner of Town Quay Park, there is a small garden dedicated to the Huguenots who came to Southampton seeking sanctuary from religious persecution in France and the Netherlands. A mulberry tree, which is a symbol of the silk industry brought to the city by the Huguenots, shades plants of French origin. A nearby plaque, donated by the Women's Gas Federation for its opening in 1985, explains the garden's history.

In their small settlement at Southampton eighty people died of plague in 1665. This devastating illness, which swept the countryside in the 1660s, killed 800 English people that year in the nearby town.

Spitalfields and London

Spitalfields, nowadays a district of London, above all is the area associated with the Huguenots. Its historic association with the silk industry was established by those French Protestant refugees who settled in this area after the Revocation of the Edict of Nantes in 1685. By residing here, outside the bounds of the City of London, they hoped to avoid the restrictive legislation of the City Guilds. The Huguenots brought little with them apart from their skills, and an Order in Council of 16 April 1687 raised £200,000 (a considerable sum of money in those days) for the relief of their poverty. In December 1687, the first report of the committee set up to administer the funds, reported that 13,050 French refugees were settled in London, primarily around Spitalfields, but also in the nearby settlements of Bethnal Green, Shoreditch, Whitechapel and Mile End New Town.

The late seventeenth and eighteenth centuries saw an estate of well-appointed terraced houses, built to accommodate the master weavers controlling the silk industry, and grand urban mansions built around the newly created Spital Square. In 1860, a treaty was established with France, allowing the import of cheaper French silks. This undercut the work of the Spitalfields' weavers and left many there and in Bethnal Green impoverished. New trades such as furniture- and boot-making came to the area, and the large windowed Huguenot houses were found suitable for tailoring; attracting a new population of Jewish refugees drawn to live and work in the textile industry.

As with Spitalfields and Bethnal Green, the late seventeenth and early eighteenth-century Protestant refugees to Soho were driven by religious conviction and dominated the area. The French Protestant Church was established in Soho Square and to this day is the only remaining Huguenot church in London.

Following the French Revolution and the Terror, the population in the West End of London was substantially mixed with French Catholic priests and political refugees of a very different stamp. By 1801, around 5,600 priests and 4,000 lay French Catholics could be counted as British residents. Their community centred on Soho to the south, and Fitzrovia just to the north of Oxford Street. In the mid-eighteenth century, William Maitland could claim: 'Many parts of this parish so greatly abound with French that it is an easy matter for a stranger to imagine himself in France'.

Thorney

Refugees were invited to settle in Thorney, in the Cambridgeshire fenlands, because of their expertise in maintaining drained land, which could be cultivated and farmed. Moving to and settling in Thorney offered advantages: Oliver Cromwell declared that if they bought or farmed lands the newcomers were accounted as 'free denizens of the Commonwealth'. In a proclamation by Cromwell, the settlers were given extra rights, including some tax relief and exemptions from military service overseas for forty years. They worshipped in the ruins of Thorney Abbey, where there is a marble memorial tablet on the north wall inscribed to Ezekiel Danois of Compiegne, France, the first minister of the Huguenot colony which fled to England and settled in Thorney. He was at Thorney Abbey for twenty-one years, and buried there, aged 54, in 1674. Huguenot pastors continued to minister at Thorney until 1715.

The settlement had two further influxes. The first was caused by Queen Elizabeth who 'sent' the Artois Walloons from Southampton to Thorney. The second influx was caused by the French Church in London in about 1685. They moved a group of Huguenots from the south up into the Thorney area to 'take part in that congregation' and to 'bolster' the population. The real reason was that the French Church had been having trouble with the Walloons at Thorney and Norwich for a long time. The Walloons, originally from the Spanish Netherlands, spoke a different language called Romand. It was not a patois or dialect of French but their own dedicated tongue: a Romance language akin to French but said to be much older. They did not want pastors venturing forth from London to preach in French and had been recruiting their own clerics, who shared their language, from the former Spanish Netherlands.

The French church in London tried to stem this practice by moving some of their people to Thorney.

The Huguenots were immensely skilled people and included amongst their ranks: silk weavers, hatmakers, goldsmiths, printers, bookbinders, watchmakers, jewellers, papermakers, gunsmiths and cabinetmakers. These skills and their hard work were injected into the British economy with a multiplier effect on other businesses. The loss of these skills in France was immeasurable. Protestant areas in France suffered drastically. The towns of Dijon, Tours, Nimes and Rouen lost half their workers and Lyons lost all but 3,000 of their 12,000 silk workers. Some observers feared that Louis XIV had committed economic suicide by driving away his most productive artisans and entrepreneurs. At Versailles, Duc de Saint Simon confided in his diary that Louis had 'depopulated a quarter of the kingdom, ruined its commerce and weakened it in all its parts'. Similar sentiments had been expressed by the Duchess of Parma to her brother, Phillip II, concerning the flight of the Walloons from the Spanish Netherlands.

There was no shortage of support for those fleeing Catholic France and its cruel leader, Louis XIV. The support came from the churches and charities based in London and beyond. The Bishop of London preached a sermon exhorting all churches to contribute to these poor refugees by door-knocking and collecting individual contributions in their own parishes. This was in addition to monies the church would contribute centrally.

The crown introduced a system of payments according to size of Protestant refugee population which continued for many years.

Of these refugees who fled Louis XIV, most were successful and many were high achievers. One of the boys who'd been hidden in the wine barrels (referred to previously), Henri de Portal, took the English name Henry Portal and opened a paper mill in 1712. Within a decade had made his fortune through the banknote paper contract.

Sir John Houblon became the first governor of the Bank of England which had been set up in 1694 and to which Huguenots contributed 10 per cent of its capital.

John Dollond of Dollond and Aitchison was the son of silk weavers but in 1750 he set up his firm of opticians, which continued in operation until 2009, when it was taken over by Boots.

There is no doubt that a number of Huguenots were highly successful in terms of building flourishing business and securing positions of authority in a variety of institutions.

It is estimated that the Walloons and Strangers who came to Britain from the 1560s onwards number around 10,000 although there is no way of discovering if any returned home. Those Huguenots who arrived after the events of 1685 onwards number between 40,000 and 50,000.

From those numbers, it is reasonable to estimate that they will have thousands and thousands of descendants. The Huguenot Museum estimates that up to one in six people now living are their descendants. Through the growing popularity of family history research many new stories are coming to light.

It is important to remember that many such names abound in Ireland since during the time of the Huguenots' flight the country was a colony of Britain. In 1674, the British Parliament passed an Act giving letters of naturalisation to all Huguenot and Walloon refugees living in Ireland at the time.

One well-known Irish person bearing a Huguenot name is war correspondent Orla Guerin. Her sister Veronica Guerin, an investigative journalist, was tragically gunned down outside Dublin in 1996 by drug barons whose corruption she was investigating.

Some Huguenot and Walloon names have been anglicised. For example, the Flemish name De Groot became Groot and L'Oiseau took its direct English translation as Bird.

Mention has already been made of the Portal family who were awarded the first contract to produce banknotes in the 1720s and Sir John Houblon who became the first governor of the Bank of England. The lexicon of Huguenot names is quite extensive including such names as Furneaux, Devereux, Noquet, Bosanquet and Bosquet.

Andrew Noquet is known to the author as a retired worker from the Plymouth Foyer. His sister has carried out extensive family research and located the Noquet family as descendants of Huguenot weavers in Spitalfields in the eighteenth century. Thomas Arno is another acquaintance who lives in Bideford, Devon but his heritage derives from his seafaring ancestor from the north-east of England. Also named Thomas, he was a shipwright and a Huguenot and was buried in the graveyard of St Mary's Church (adjacent to Whitby Abbey) in 1867. Other members of the Arno family are recorded in the church register dating back to the eighteenth century and are also buried there. The author also discovered that her dentist, Richard Caradine was of Huguenot descent.

Derek Jacobi's past was researched for the television programme *Who Do You Think You Are?* From his own upbringing in the East End he has become a talented and successful actor. Tracing his family roots, the programme discovered an ancestor who was a Huguenot and financier at the court of Louis X. Having to conceal his religion, he was eventually uncovered and imprisoned in a prison in the Loire Valley. Managing to escape he made his way to England where at the age of 70 he married a Huguenot lady called Salome de la Bastide and fathered a son before his death.

Interestingly, Salome's brother was recruited to fight with William of Orange against Catholic armies in Ireland at the Battle of the Boyne in 1690. Many Huguenot exiles fought alongside William at this iconic battle.

Tobias Furneaux (1735–81) who was born in 'Swilly' (now North Prospect) on the outskirts of Plymouth was of Huguenot descent. He was a naval man who accompanied Captain Cook on several voyages and is credited to be the first man to navigate the globe in two directions. In 1755, he was involved in an expedition with Cook, trying to find a southern habitable continent. Finding those parts too cold for habitation he turned north and discovered the coasts of Tasmania, which he proceeded to map in detail. His voyage home took him past Australia and New Zealand.

And finally, the recent episode of *Poldark*, in series five, featured a certain Joseph Merceron, a character in this work of fiction, who is described as a powerful and enterprising magistrate with connections and influence throughout the social and political tiers of London. In fact, there was an actual man of the same name who was a wealthy Huguenot and magistrate whose money was gained corruptly: a case of fiction copying reality.

Chapter 3

The Poor Palatines

T he year 1709 saw the arrival of another group of Protestant
refugees to English shores.[1] These people arrived from the
Palatine area of Germany. The Palatine consisted of lands of the
Count Palatine, a title held by a leading secular prince of the Holy Roman
Empire. Geographically, the Palatinate was divided between two small
territorial clusters: the Rhenish, or Lower, Palatinate and the Upper
Palatinate. The Rhenish Palatinate included lands on both sides of the
middle Rhine River between its Main and Neckar tributaries. Its capital
until the eighteenth century was Heidelberg.

During the early reformation, in certain areas of the Palatine the
people had adopted Calvinism as their creed. During the War of the
Grand Alliance (1689–97), the troops of the French Catholic monarch,
Louis XIV (the fourteenth, born 1638 and who died in 1715), ravaged the
Rhenish Palatinate, causing many Germans and Palatines to emigrate.
The French Army laid waste to their state and the resulting destruction
of their crops. Following Louis's expulsion of the French Huguenots we
see that this 'Sun King' was a monarch who created refugees in his wake.

Unlike the Huguenots and their predecessors, the Walloon refugees,
the Palatines were largely agricultural workers with few skills beyond
their work on the land. Hence they were dubbed the 'Poor Palatines':
both poor in economic terms and to be pitied for their plight.

The first group arriving were led by a man called Joshua Kochental.
His aim was to lead these people to a new life in America and he managed
to obtain money from the British government for this purpose. People
following hoped for a similar supportive response. Unfortunately, events
did not follow this pattern.

The Poor Palatines were interesting in that they were the first group of
refugees whose presence caused a clear political split regarding attitudes
and support. The Whigs favoured support for them and, whilst in

government, introduced an Act of Naturalisation: the Foreign Protestants Naturalisation Act of 1708.

Interestingly, as an aside, the Act was actually passed on 23 March 1709, which was still considered part of the year 1708 in the British calendar of the time. It was originally designed to assist the Huguenots fleeing France but once passed in Parliament it was used to assist the Poor Palatines. A well-known supporter of the Palatines was Daniel Defoe and Whig supporters were happy to offer financial support.

It is estimated that some 13,000 Poor Palatines arrived in the six months between May and November 1709. Initially some 900 of the early arrivals were provided with housing and food by sympathetic wealthy gentlemen. Unlike the earlier arrivals of the Huguenots, most were not absorbed into existing communities but had to be housed in large tented encampments at Blackheath and Camberwell on the south-eastern fringes of London. In this respect they became the forerunners of so many refugee camps across the modern world.

There was generosity shown to the Poor Palatines: in Stoke Newington the parish built four houses for them.[2] The fact that Daniel Defoe lived in that area may have something to do with this outcome. The actual buildings are long gone but interestingly the name 'Palatine' still survives – in a way acting as a testament to their existence – in Stoke Newington, which has both a Palatine Avenue and a Palatine Road.

Contrary to the Whigs, the Tories opposed the Poor Palatines and were vocal in expressing that opposition. Concerns were expressed about the threat the Palatine refugees might pose if allowed to remain in Britain. Many were poor, unskilled labourers, and it was argued that they would add nothing to the nation's prosperity but instead reduce work and wages for their British counterparts.

We have seen that one vocal supporter of the Palatines' right to remain was Daniel Defoe (1660 to 1731: journalist, pamphleteer and the author of many books including *Robinson Crusoe*). His political periodical, *A Review of the State of the Nation*, argued that British tradesmen and labourers had nothing to fear and that the newcomers would enhance rather than damage the 'publick wealth'. Giving the Palatines the right to acquire citizenship via naturalisation was seen as being inclusive and welcoming to them. He also recommended settling the Palatines in sparsely inhabited regions to develop the land for agriculture.

But other voices were less welcoming. A contemporary pamphlet, *The Palatines Catechism*, sets out some typical elements of the debate in a fictional dialogue between an 'English tradesman' and a 'High-Dutchman' (probably a German in modern parlance). Visiting the refugees' camp, the 'High-Dutchman' admires their 'Diligence and Industry' and argues that Christian charity demands they should be supported and helped to settle in Britain. The Englishman sees only disorder and outlandish habits in the camp and is suspicious of the Palatines' motives for coming; he declares that, 'charity ought to begin at home', and that Britain should help her own numerous poor before taking in those of other countries. This is a much replayed argument by people who only remember their own poor as part of declining to help others.

He also fears that, if the Palatines are given assistance, they will repay it by exploiting their benefactors once they are settled. Ironically, this fictional debate, like many of the real ones, ignored the fact that most of the refugees had no desire to remain in Britain long term.

However, when the Tories came to power, later in 1709, they stopped any programmes the Whigs had instigated to help the Poor Palatines and cancelled the Act of Naturalisation. Ultimately, they banned the arrival of more boats with people from the Palatine. This has clear resonance with the actions being taken against refugees in the Mediterranean today.

Previously we have seen that all the earlier Protestant refugees received support from the monarchy. Any opposition was by other skilled workers who saw their livelihoods threatened. Queen Anne (who was Queen of England, Scotland and Ireland between 8 March 1702 and 1 May 1707, and then henceforth, following the Act of Union, Queen of Great Britain and Ireland until her death in 1714), initially supported the Palatines but as the arguments raged her support waned. It was claimed that not all those arriving from the continent were Protestant refugees but rather some were Catholics from that area pushed out by economic circumstances. Redefining a group's religion or ethnicity can be used to scapegoat them. As more Palatines continued to land, it was argued that there were simply too many people to help.

This argument was misplaced since most Palatines wished to follow their brethren to America and did not want a long stay in the tented cities or indeed in Britain.

Some were dispersed within Britain; Liverpool and parts of Lancashire absorbed some, as did Perth in Scotland.

Persuaded by a committee of powerful Irish Protestant landlords, the queen agreed to send some of the Palatine peoples to Ireland. She was told that they would help to develop farming land and importantly act as a Protestant bulwark against Irish Catholicism. Until independence in the 1920s, Ireland was, of course, part of Britain. Not all were successful: some returned to England and some went to seek work in Dublin. But of around 130 families who went to work on the lands of Sir Thomas Southwell near Rathkeale, they and the land prospered. Descendants of these German refugees can still be found in the Limerick county area to this day.

Eventually about 3,000 of the Palatines were granted their wishes and were allowed passage to the Americas (at this time still controlled by the British state). It is debatable that this was as they had wished, since the contract that they had unwittingly entered into was to make them indentured labourers.

Of interest there was a society established in Rathkeale, County Limerick, for all Palatine descendants in Ireland, which has its own heritage centre.[3]

Chapter 4

The French Revolution Refugees and Other European Exiles of the Nineteenth Century

P erhaps the most momentous change in Europe prior to the nineteenth century was the upheaval caused by the French Revolution in 1789. Years of bad harvests in the 1780s, exacerbated by deregulation of the grain industry, caused great hardship amongst ordinary people who were enraged by the privileges of the aristocracy and established churches. The ideas fermented during these turbulent years spread across France and into radical philosophies brought into this country.

Revolutionary ideas of the Enlightenment challenging the status quo of the establishment – the monarchy, the church and the aristocracy – which had been evolving and unfurling over several years, came to a head in 1789.

France was ruled by an absolute government. The king had all the political powers. Anyone who criticised the government could be arrested and put in prison without trial. Louis XVI was king at the time of the French Revolution and was more interested in hunting than governing France. He and his Austrian queen, Marie Antoinette, lived an extravagant life at the Palace of Versailles. They did not really care about the state of their country.

In that first year following the revolution, feudalism was abolished, the Bastille was attacked and the March of the Women on Versailles forced the Royal Court to return back to Paris. The Declaration of the Rights of Man was published.

But it was the subsequent revolutionary tribunals which tried and condemned to death aristocrats, deemed enemies of the state, which caused people to flee.

Between 16,000 and 40,000 people were executed, causing fear and panic in those of the same aristocratic class. The sight of the tumbrils (two-wheeled carts) taking aristocrats to be guillotined has become the substance of books and cinematographic images in films but there was nothing glamorous for those terrified people awaiting their fate. It was not only the aristocrat who suffered death but ultimately anyone considered counter-revolutionary. Priests and anyone considered supporters of the old religion were under such threat.

For those living in the west of the country, in and around Nantes, another form of terror lay in store. From the autumn of 1793 to the spring of 1794, Jean-Baptiste Carrier was put in charge of the area and given carte blanche to round up alleged counter-revolutionaries. This started with priests, then moved on to anyone suspected of opposing the revolution. His chosen method of execution was by mass drowning.[1] He had rounded up 160 priests in the summer and imprisoned them on the decks of a barge positioned on the mouth of the river Loire. Baking in the summer sun, they suffered greatly before being taken to a nearby prison. That 'respite' was not to last, since on a cold November night he took them back to the Loire to a barge he had had specially customised by carpenters. Once out in the deep estuary, trap doors were opened: sending the men to a watery grave. On that occasion, three priests managed to swim to the shore but their efforts were in vain as they were picked up and shackled to be taken to the barge the next night.

On 4 December, Carrier met with other officials and drew up a list of people to be arrested and subjected to the same treatment. Families, including children, were not exempt.

On at least one occasion, drunken soldiers ignored any kind of list and rampaged into the cells, grabbing people at random.

It is said they took pleasure in enforcing 'underwater marriages' which involved tying a priest and a nun together face to face before pushing them into the freezing waters of the estuary.

By May of 1794 the drownings ceased. It was estimated up to 4,800 had died under Carrier's watch and another 2,000 using his methods. Carrier was recalled to Paris, where he was questioned about this particularly gruesome form of execution, which he tried to deny. Ultimately, he was simply not believed and his life was ended under the blade of the guillotine.

The baptism of George Marie Bertrand, a Catholic child whose parents had fled to Plymouth, was recorded in a Stonehouse church.[2] It is not difficult to imagine that living close to Nantes they had taken the often treacherous route through the Bay of Biscay to seek sanctuary in Devon from the terror perpetuated by Jean-Baptise Carrier.

It is estimated that 1 per cent of the French population fled (the French population in 1784 was 24.8 million); many to Germany, the Low Countries, Switzerland and the US. However, for those living in Normandy and the north-west of the country, England, and particularly London, was their place of refuge. An added incentive was that the MP John Wilmot raised funds to help the refugees, and the father of Fanny Burney, an English satirical author who wrote the novel *Evelina* in 1778, gave succour to the most needy widows and orphans.

Not all of the refugees were from an aristocratic background and some fled with nothing. However, the aristocrats themselves usually had to flee leaving all their belongings behind; the reality of their personal circumstances meant that they were more likely to have wealthy friends in this country.

Most settled in London and primarily in Soho, an area which was quite culturally French. There was a French hotel and in Soho's Poland Street there was a *Prix Fixe* restaurant run by a French chef, which would have made the exiles feel at home. Money was a constant worry but where people could, they continued trades practised at home.

Soho had long been a haven for French exiles, housing many thousands of Frenchmen from the last mass migration of Huguenots after the Revocation of the Edict of Nantes. This community made it easier for the French refugees to settle in. However, having left with virtually no possessions, life was not easy for these exiles who had been used to a comfortable life. Most people just picked back up the trades they had in France, and aristocrats found themselves having to seek employment for the first time in years. Those who were educated often offered their services as instructors in French, dancing, and fencing.

Those refugees who had no usable skills or ability to work as labourers turned to crime. The truly elite émigrés settled in Marylebone, Richmond and Hampstead where the politics were extremely royalist. In contrast, émigrés from the lower classes of society often settled in St

Pancras and St George's Fields. Both of these areas facilitated the ability of the émigrés to maintain their Catholic faith. In St Pancras, émigrés were allowed to use the Anglican church, and for occasions of particular significance, they were allowed to worship without any interference from the Anglican clergy. In St George's Fields, the Chapel of Notre-Dame was opened in 1796. These poorer émigrés were an eclectic group. They included widows, men wounded in war, the elderly, the ecclesiastics, and some provincial nobility, along with domestic servants. It has been noted that 'there was little that these émigrés had in common besides their misfortunes and their stoic perseverance in the absence of any alternative'. Malnutrition and poor living conditions led to an onslaught of maladies. And death did not quite put an end to the suffering, for even posthumously their families were beset with the financial burden of administering their funeral rites. To alleviate their hunger, a soup kitchen was opened in 1810 in the St Pancras area.

Refugee arrivals reached their highest in 1792, with an estimated 4,000 arriving. Concern about this eventually led to the Aliens Act of 1793, which required people to register with the authorities on arrival. It was in essence just a recording mechanism or census, with no sanctions attached such as deportation.[3]

The situation in France, from the point of view of the refugees, improved though in 1815, when the French monarchy was restored and some émigrés began to return home.

When refugees are forced to flee from their own homeland they often perform to their best. The father of Isambard Kingdom Brunel left Normandy in flight from the French Revolution. Himself an engineer, he brought his family to the south of England where Isambard was born in Portsmouth in 1806. Working with his father from an early age he became one of Britain's most successful and esteemed engineers. Among his many works are the Clifton Suspension Bridge in Bristol, the Royal Albert Bridge in Plymouth, the Great Western Railway and Paddington Station.

The French émigrés of 1789 onwards were not alone in fleeing revolutions and upheavals in their own country. And while the term 'Century of Revolution' is often used historically for the years 1603 to 1714, the nineteenth century saw many such upheavals. A rebellion in

Spain in 1823 brought refugees to Somerstown (known nowadays as Somers Town), near Camden in London and in 1827 they were recorded with Italian refugees playing football tournaments on Copenhagen Fields in Islington.[3] These refugees were supported by sympathetic authorities at a high level. In the autumn of 1828, a meeting of respectable gentlemen was held at the London Tavern. The Lord Mayor of London chaired the meeting and said: 'The persons whose destitute condition they had it in mind to relieve, were men who had been reduced to their present state of poverty in their conscientious endeavours to secure for themselves and their countrymen the advantages of a free government.' He recounted the suffering of some amongst them, including the infirm, and women and children. Many of these were bordering on destitution. Since 1823 the government had supported about 700 people. He noted that those whose fortunes had improved were in turn supporting refugees still in need.

Praise was given to a Mr Waterhouse, a coach proprietor, who conveyed refugees who had managed to travel to work from their new lodgings, often at great distances, and help them with necessities on the way.

It transpires that the contents of this story were relayed around the country in newspapers.[4] On 6 December 1828, a letter from the Mansion House in London was received by the Mayor of Plymouth. It recounted their meeting and wish to raise subscriptions across the country for these 'distressed gentlemen'. Interestingly, it further refers to them as 'unfortunate Strangers' using the terminology first used in the sixteenth century for those people from the Spanish Netherlands. The mayor then wrote to a number of the gentlemen of the town to convene a meeting. Such names as Woolcombe, Hatchard, Cookworthy and Eastlake are included in the addresses. From reading the correspondence, there is every sense that people will be disposed to contribute and the mayor mentions other towns being written to in a similar vein.

Another revolution in France, in 1830, saw 150 priests fleeing to London again. On this occasion they did not fare well and it was said that within four years half had died of privation. The remaining men needed to petition the lord mayor for alms.

Agitation for Italian unification brought further exiles to England. The most famous was Giuseppe Mazzini, who was considered the apostle of modern democracy and the inspiration for 'Young Italy', a political movement for Italian youth (under the age of 40), founded in 1831. Arriving in 1850, he had already been expelled from Piedmont, France and Switzerland.

However, in London he was able to find refuge and continue his writing and discussion with other political thinkers. He stayed there for most of the rest of his life.

It was the French Revolution of 1848 that brought people in their greatest numbers including Louis Blanc, Louis Philippe and Louis Napoleon. Louis Blanc was the first avowedly socialist French politician who favoured workers' co-operatives to help the urban poor.[5] He became part of the provisional government after the Revolution of 1848. Ultimately he was caught between the radical worker tendency and the pressures of the National Guard and was forced to flee to London. There he was able to use the collection at the British Museum to complete his History of the French Revolution.

Louis Philippe was king of France until he was dethroned by the 1848 revolution.[6] His royal connections placed him in a rather favoured position as he was befriended by a young Queen Victoria and given a house at Claremont in Surrey.

Louis Napoleon swept to power with 75 per cent of the popular vote in December 1848 after Louis Philippe had been dethroned.[7] He was a populist and was much helped by being a descendant of the original Napoleon. He continued to rule France first as king and then emperor and was thought to have been a popular reforming ruler. His downfall came with the Franco-Prussian war where he was taken prisoner by the Prussians. He spent his final three years in exile in Kent.

But it was in August 1849 that probably the most famous émigré of all, Karl Marx, came to London, having been expelled from Cologne and then Paris. The following year he brought his wife and children to live with him. Living at a variety of addresses in North London, he stayed here until his death in 1883. He was buried in Highgate Cemetery.

There was some street hostility to these foreign arrivals. But they had friends in the middle classes who wined and dined them and intellectuals like David Masson, a Scottish academic (Secretary of the Friends of Italy Society in the 1850s) who organised charity support and spoke for European liberty. Seeing common cause, the Chartists funded a barrack in Clerkenwell for Hungarian, Polish and Italian refugees. When news came through of the Paris Revolution in 1848, a meeting rose in jubilation and promptly marched on to the streets, chanting slogans.

In 1870, the terrible destruction wrought in Paris by the Franco-Prussian war and the decimation of the Commune brought around 3,000 people, including families, to British shores. It speaks well of attitudes at that time that people were admitted without any bureaucratic obstacles and welcomed with open arms. Amongst their numbers were impressionist artists who were able to take up residence mainly in London. Such well-known names as Monet, Sisley, Pissarro and Tissot made London their home for the time being, with some remaining permanently.

Prince Peter Kropotkin, the Russian anarchist, described the Union Jack as 'the flag under which so many refugees, Russian, Italian, French, Hungarian and of all nations, had found asylum'.[8] This idea of nineteenth-century tolerance towards newcomers finds support in an editorial in *The Times* of 19 January 1858, which declared: 'Every civilised people on the face of the earth must be fully aware that this country is the asylum of nations, and that it would defend the asylum to the last drop of its blood.'

These assertions receive backing from the fact that between 1826 and 1848, and 1850 and 1905, Britain did not implement any statutory restrictions upon the entry of aliens.

An explanation of this state of affairs might stress two facts. Firstly, the underlying prosperity of the Victorian period. Secondly, the relatively small numbers of refugees involved. Alliances and disputes with other European countries played a part too. The first major campaign against newcomers occurred at the end of the nineteenth century, following the large influx of Russian Jewish refugees fleeing from tsarist persecution. Their entry came at a time when Britain's decline as the major world economic power was well under way and people, fearing for their jobs and prosperity, saw any incoming group of workers as a threat to this. The campaign which led to the Aliens Act 1905 received much of its impetus from the East End of London, where many of the newcomers settled and where natives saw them as an economic, social and even a cultural threat.[9]

We might view the events of the years leading up to 1905 as setting the tone for attitudes towards refugees in twentieth-century Britain. In contrast to the open-door policy of the 1800s, the new arrivals, with their strange religious practices and overcrowded living conditions, became the scapegoats of the 'British Brothers' League', which was established in 1901 by Conservative MPs and began an anti-aliens' campaign. Ostensibly it was a working-class anti-immigration body. In 1905, they commanded a meeting of around 5,000 people in the East End of London and it was this campaign, primarily targeting Jewish refugees from Russia, which led to the introduction of the Aliens Act of 1905. It occurred in the aftermath of the Boer War/Second South African War (1899–1902), where soldiers roused to patriotism had arrived home to find there was little support for them, having served their country, apart from charitable handouts or the workhouse.

Chapter 5

The Portuguese Refugees in Plymouth

T he story of refugees to this country is in many ways a hidden history. That approximately 3,000 Portuguese refugees were lodging in the author's adopted town of Plymouth in 1828 would be a great surprise to many Plymothians. These refugees had fled from their home country in five overloaded boats. Their arrival in St Ives, Cornwall, a seemingly unlikely port of call, was probably the first place they could land safely in such overloaded, leaky vessels.[1] The willingness to put to sea in such unseaworthy boats was a measure of their fear. They were fearful of a civil war between two would-be kings, Pedro and Miguel, who vied for the throne, vacant upon their father's death. They were supporters of Pedro and had been involved in an uprising against Miguel and the repression that he was unleashing.

St Ives then had a population of 6,000 people living in small overcrowded cottages which gave little room to accommodate others. Hence it was decided that they should be moved onto Plymouth, which housed military barracks and large warehouses. They were taken by boat to Plymouth, where warehouses had been opened for them and accommodation arranged on board four docked ships. Most were from a professional class and many had a military background. The refugees were put in six groupings as follows:[2]

First: War Department general staff;
Second: First line officers;
Third: Second Line Officers, volunteers and orderlies;
Fourth: Civil servants;
Fifth: Priests, merchants, landlords, physicians and other liberal professions;
Sixth: First and second line enlisted soldiers, volunteers and servants.

Thus their statuses on land were clearly defined.

The refugees favoured the young exiled Queen of Portugal, Dona Maria, who had arrived in Britain and was being taken around the country to meet supporters. (Dona Maria II of Portugal was queen from 1826 to 1828, and later restored to the throne from 1834 until her death in 1853, aged 43 years.)

Strangely, she wasn't brought to Plymouth but perhaps her minders felt she could not tolerate the crowds.

The refugees were given a daily meal valued at 6*d* and it seems all were paid the equivalent of military payments in Portugal. For those of the lowest rank (the sixth grade which included first and second lines enlisted soldiers, volunteers, servants etc.), their pay only amounted to 14*s* a month and this forced some of them to beg locally.

This was unpopular and the *Devonport Telegraph* opined that it was only 'merchants, innkeepers and prostitutes rather than respectable people who liked the refugees'.

The archival evidence available at the Devon Heritage Centre and Plymouth and West Devon Records Office suggests, interestingly, that many gentlemen felt sympathy with them. A Mr Acland, who was visiting the town, said that some are 'heavily moustachioed but some have shaved' and 'are changing their regimentals for an English cut coat'.[3] He also notes that many are superior to 'his own countrymen' and now speak English tolerably well. These comments were made when the refugees had been in the country for four or five months.

Whilst in town the refugees staged a play. This was to celebrate the visit of the young Queen Dona Maria to the West Country, although it should be noted that she didn't come to Plymouth. At the barracks, they constructed a stage and performed a comedy called *Elvira* by Jao de Mutos. The Portuguese Viscount Palmella had the production of the play closed down because he thought it satirised him and the brigadier. This did not dampen the dramatic aspirations of the refugees who proceeded to perform a serious play approved by the authorities. *Cantano* was staged on 24 October, and subsequently on 1 and 23 December at the Royal Hotel and Theatre.[4] The Earl of Morley, owner of the theatre, attended this performance. At the end of November 1828, when news came that the refugees were about to be moved, ten of the 'great and good' of the city wrote to the mayor asking for a meeting:

We the undersigned, having learned that it is in contemplation to DISPERSE the PORTUGUESE REFUGEES resident here whereby their sufferings would be still further aggravated; and feeling that the cause of Constitutional Liberty for which these sufferings have been incurred, and their good conduct during their residence entitle them to our sympathy whilst their presence is rather beneficial than injurious to the town, respectfully request that your Worship will be pleased to call a PUBLIC MEETING of the inhabitants to consider of the propriety of expressing their sentiments to His Majesty's government and of using our endeavours to avert the calamity with which they are threatened.[5]

This message was relayed to the Home Secretary, Mr Robert Peel, but by early January 1829, it seems that they could not forestall the wishes of the Portuguese. The young Portuguese queen, who had toured the country whilst staying in Britain, had been proclaimed ruler in Terceira on the Portuguese island territory of the Azores and required the refugees, most of whom were soldiers, to be taken there to reinforce the garrison. In this she was backed by the Brazilian ambassador and Viscount Palmella. She had not bothered to visit the refugees in Plymouth but now they were under her orders. The *Spectator* journal tells us the government here was not keen on this plan but the refugees were not their nationals and therefore not their responsibility.

Throughout the time, from June 1828, Wellington was prime minister. He was an ardent supporter of the would-be king, Miguel, and when he heard the refugees had been sent to support the ousted Queen Dona Maria in the Azores he had the sent the British navy to prevent that from happening.

On 17 January 1829, 4 ships carrying 700 Portuguese set sail.[6] There was a conflict at the heart of government and it seems it was known that the British navy was to attempt to stop them. The refugees were instructed to attempt a landing but to give themselves up if that was not possible. Within six or seven months they had been involved in an uprising, taken an overcrowded boat to St Ives, been accommodated quite poorly in Plymouth and now were likely to be confronted by the navy of the very country that had given them shelter. The ship was said to be sailing nominally to Brazil but it was supposed that the Azores would be their first port of call. However, in parallel, British navy vessels had set out to impede their progress.

On 7 February the American ship *James Cropper* was nearing the island of Terceira assisting the refugees.[7] A report came through by the end of the month, stating that half the refugees had landed and that the Americans would rescue the rest under convoy.

In early March, the British frigate was unceremoniously recalled and in Britain and across Europe there was heavy criticism of Britain's actions in trying to stop the refugees landing. Sympathy for the refugees was rekindled.

This piece of hidden history unlocked a mystery stemming from a personal find twenty years ago. When the author's children were young, they attended a summer play scheme on the Brickfields site in Devonport. Brickfields was a running track and sports' field which lay directly next to the Raglan Barracks. The boys managed to unearth a heavy coin which, on examination, proved to be Portuguese dated 1828. It had a reeded edge pattern and was inscribed with the name of King Miguel. Naturally the author tried to find out more and took it to Plymouth Museum where they were able to show a record in a coin book but could offer no explanation as to why it was found at that Devonport location.

Now it is known why the 3,000 Portuguese refugees who were in the town for that brief period, from the autumn 1828 to early 1829. It is known that the coin belonged to one of them and would have been a great loss to him. Perhaps he was involved in a fight or it slipped out of his pocket unnoticed. Maybe he was one of the 'moustachioed gentlemen'. Maybe he was one of the actors in the two different plays. Whatever is the truth, this research has helped identify the Portuguese refugees of Plymouth and a fragment of this man's life from approximately 190 years ago.

Chapter 6

A Story of Nineteenth- and Twentieth- Century Persecution

Jewish people have long been the subject of persecution. With a religion and practices considered different from mainstream Christian practice they could easily become the focus of suspicion. In twelfth-century England, a myth that took hold was that of the 'blood libel', which became one of the earliest forms of anti-Semitic thought. This alleged that the Jews would murder Christian children to use their blood for Jewish rituals. A boy called William of Norwich was killed with an injury to the head and it was said that this resembled the crown of thorns that Jesus was made to wear at the Crucifixion. Another view held contemporary Jews guilty of that Crucifixion. Unfair and wrong as these beliefs were, it is possible to see how in a credulous age they took hold and were used to stir up violence against Jewish people. William the Conqueror had brought some Jewish officials from France with him because he needed access to money for constructing castles and other works. Jewish people were allowed to lend money, a practice forbidden to Christians. Increasingly, the native Christians felt the Jews should convert, as their religion was not acceptable. In the northern town of York, communal riots broke out in 1190. Some 150 people of the Jewish community retreated to Clifford's Tower, then a wooden structure at the top of mound. Scared and isolated, the Jews fearing forced conversion and violent attack, began to kill themselves. In each family the father killed the children, followed by his wife, and finally himself. The mob then burnt down the remaining wooden structure. Subsequently, Edward I expelled all Jews in 1290 and none returned officially until 1656, under the rule of Cromwell.

In 1498, Catholic Ferdinand and Isabella of Aragon expelled all Jews and Muslims from Spain.[1] Most went to other European countries and Turkey but a few Jewish people, who had converted and were known as Marannos or Conversos, made it to England.

In Europe, Jews were persecuted in the eighteenth century. In 1740, Empress Marie Theresa threatened to expel all Jews during the War of Austrian Succession from Moravia and Bohemia.

In 1768, a terrible massacre took place in the region of Latvia.[2] Twenty thousand Jewish people, along with some Polish people, were herded into the town of Uman by Haidamacks (paramilitary bands that disrupted the social order in Polish Ukraine during the eighteenth century). The name originated from the Turkish word *haida* meaning 'move on!') The Jewish people fought bravely but eventually were forced to retreat into the synagogue, whereupon their attackers blasted the building with canon fire, leaving no survivors. Such targeted annihilations created terror in the Jewish populations of central Europe.

When Russia acquired parts of Poland on its eastern border, it created an area known as the Pale of Settlement in 1804. All Jews were required to live in this area, thus restricting their movement and their life chances. They were expelled from the villages since it was believed that they fomented trouble there. They were also ordered not to lease lands from the nobles and not to run taverns, as it was believed that this would give them access to many people and allow them to extend their influence.

Life continued to be difficult through the nineteenth century, until in 1881 an event occurred which created panic in the population: Tsar Nicholas of Russia was assassinated and blame was heaped on the Jews. Pogroms resumed in earnest and many were forced to flee, travelling to England and the USA.

Many of those who came to England ended up in London and crowded into the East End, where there was already a sizeable Jewish population. Unable to work on the Sabbath and without a command of English, they went to work for existing Jewish masters who ran the sweated trades in garment-making. The working conditions were poor, adversely affecting the workers' health. Newly arrived members of the Jewish community stayed in lodges dedicated to Jewish immigrants.

There was already a long-established community of Jewish businessmen in Britain, and especially in London. The prosperous middle-class and elite Jews clustered heavily in the West End of the metropolis, leaving the East End to the poor. The established Jewish community wished to welcome the newcomers as part of their desire to regulate their movements. There was a Jewish Board of Guardians separate from the statutorily appointed Board of Guardians. In 1854, a Jewish soup kitchen had been started in the East End. It was to provide soup, bread and meat twice a week for Jews arriving with no money. It was expected to be needed until new arrivals became integrated but it continued to exist and in the end was used for the sick and elderly in the community

The Board of Guardians was dominated by an Anglo-Jewish financial elite who organised and controlled charitable assistance as part of a plan to provide poor immigrant Jews with marketable skills and allow them to become part of the prosperous Jewish middle class. The incoming Jewish community retained many aspects of their culture in the East End of London. The wealthy resident members of the Jewish community wanted these newcomers to conform and attempted to control them. They were unhappy at the lack of respect to organised Jewry shown by the newcomers. Indeed, they tried to dissuade this increased immigration. Attempts were made to organise the new arrivals and to assert some authority.

A Poor Jews Shelter was set up and a Jewish Association for the Protection of Women and Girls. A little later, a Jewish Lads' Brigade was set up and the Brady Street club for working boys. Despite those measures to keep an eye on Jewish youth there were still problems. Hence, by 1901 it was felt necessary to set up an Industrial School for Jewish boys of criminal intent.

During the last decades of the nineteenth century, the influx of foreign Jewish people was seen as a problem – an indeterminate part of a social crisis affecting the metropolis.[3] The medical profession was tremendously exercised by the threats to public health posed by congestion in such a small area of the East End. The *Lancet* undertook its own special investigation and in 1884 (just three years after the real immigration started) reported that 30,000 Jews now 'huddled together in districts that were already overcrowded'. There was a huge concern about the congested conditions which could lead to the spread of disease, and that sweated working conditions likewise would lead to exhaustion and illness. It was also becoming increasingly apparent that ghetto communities, which largely communicated in Yiddish, would become cut off from the mainstream. Gradually some small steps were taken, such as

giving some policemen Yiddish lessons and helping with the completion
of the census.

There were those in the Jewish Community who wanted to organise
and campaign on these issues.[4] In 1889, at the time of the Great Dock
Strike, many other workers struck to fight their conditions. And those
conditions were harsh in the extreme. The clothing workers slaved for
fourteen to eighteen hours a day, six days a week with many on piece-
work rather than regular wages. They organised a strike committee and
printed leaflets demanding a twelve-hour day, with breaks for tea and
dinner outside their workplace, trade union rates for work on military
garments, and an end to the practice of giving workers items to finish
overnight. Most of the 8,000 workers were recent Jewish immigrants
from the Russian Empire.

Impoverished Jewish immigrant workers had already shown their
capacity for militant action in March 1889, when 3,000 of them marched
on Chief Rabbi Adler's Duke Street synagogue, having asked him to
deliver a sermon on sweated labour, unemployment and the demand
for an eight-hour day. Adler refused and absented himself. There were
ugly confrontations with the police near the synagogue, and later on in
Whitechapel.

The Guild of Master Tailors attempted to starve employees back
to work as the strike committee struggled to sustain the idle workers'
families. Four weeks into the dispute, the strike fund was so depleted
that cutters, pressers and basters faced the prospect of returning to work
having gained nothing. The committee made one final effort to replenish
the fund. A delegation headed to the Wade Arms pub in Poplar, home
of the Docks Strike Committee, where the committee agreed to donate
£100, the largest single subscription the tailors received. With the strike
fund refreshed, the employers now became increasingly anxious and,
in early October, they caved in. Solidarity from Irish Catholic dockers
resulted in victory for these immigrant Jewish tailors.

That cross-communal solidarity was cemented two months later,
when a Federation of East London Labour Unions was launched at Mile
End's Great Assembly Hall. However, the union was severely tested in
the troubled early years of the twentieth century, as thousands of factory
workers and local unemployed were won over to a populist anti-immigrant

organisation called the British Brothers' League (BBL), led by local Tory MPs Major William Evans-Gordon and Samuel Forde West.

The British Brothers League, which has been mentioned in Chapter 4, stirred resentment against the Jewish immigrants who were said to take the jobs of locals and cause bad housing in ways not dissimilar to the fascists of the 1930's and more recently the British National Party.

Evans-Gordon wanted to ensure no further immigration and stirred things up politically for his own ends. He called mass meetings in the East End, one attracting 4,000 people and a petition which collected 45,000 signatures. This was at the time when the Boer War was ending and jingoism was rife with returning troops parading following a victorious war. The level of 'noise' he made ensured a Royal Commission on Alien Immigration was set up in 1902. The report was generally favourable to the Jewish people but not on the question of overcrowding.

Classically, it was the immigrants living in the area who were blamed for the poor housing rather than their landlords. Ultimately the agitation led to the passing of the Aliens Act, the first ever piece of legislation to control immigration into the country. It did not ban all immigration but gave powers to officers at the ports to stop people from entering if they did not have the means, unless they were fleeing religious or political persecution. What guidelines the immigration officers had to judge these matters is not stated. The legislation was strengthened at the beginning of the First World War and repealed in 1919. But the Aliens Act had laid down a marker: the concept that people could be prevented from entering the country and that in its operation it might catch people who were fleeing persecution.

Jewish activists formed an Aliens' Defence League that held public meetings countering the British Brothers' League's propaganda. Their more long-term response was to build their own secular institutions to strengthen immigrant Jewish working-class lives, such as the Jubilee Street Club and Workers Institute in 1906 and the Arbeiter Ring (Workers Circle) in 1909.

These radical initiatives, built from the grassroots, often put them in conflict with more conservative elements in the Jewish community but they provided sustenance and hope to all who used them.

Chapter 7

The First World War and
Germany Invades Belgium

When the Belgian government refused passage to the German army in August 1914, their wishes were overridden and the German army advanced into their homeland. It proved to be an essential element of the German military strategy to confront the French army in Eastern France. Belgian neutrality had been guaranteed by the Treaty of London signed on 19 April 1839 and this was underwritten by both Prussia and Britain. The German Chancellor, Theobald von Bethmann-Hollweg, said, however, that it was simply a 'scrap of paper to be ignored'. This precipitative action was, of course, the spur for Britain declaring war on Germany on 4 August 1914.

Expecting little resistance from the Belgians, the Germans had to fight hard to capture the south-eastern city of Liege.[1] Their response to the firing within the city was to accuse people from local villages of being snipers and to execute them summarily. Most were young men of military age but women, children and even the elderly were shot. Overall the Germans were responsible for the deaths of 23,700 Belgian civilians, 6,000 of whom were killed and 17,700 died during their expulsion, deportation or whilst in prison or sentenced to death by the German martial court. They caused a further 10,400 civilians to have permanent but non-fatal injuries and a further 22,700 civilians to become temporary invalids. In addition 18,296 children became war orphans. Military losses were 26,338 people who were killed, or who died from injuries or accidents and a further 14,029 people died from disease or went missing.

The Germans also humiliated the populace by forcing them to cheer the occupying forces and publicly mistreating dignitaries such as priests and mayors.

In some places, particularly Liege, Andenne and Leuven, there is evidence that the violence against civilians was premeditated. However, in Dinant, the German army also believed the inhabitants were as dangerous as the soldiers themselves. German troops, afraid of Belgian guerrilla fighters, burned homes and executed civilians throughout eastern and central Belgium, including Aarschot (156 killed), Andenne (211 killed), Seilles and Tamines (383 killed), and Dinant (674 killed). The victims included men, women, and children.

In the Province of Brabant, nuns were ordered to strip naked under the pretext that they might be spies or men in disguise. There is no evidence that these nuns were sexually violated but the fear and humiliation would have been terrible for women used to a cloistered life. In and around Aarschot, however, between 19 August and the recapture of the town by 9 September, women were repeatedly victimised. Rape was nearly as ubiquitous as murder, arson and looting.

The small town of Dolhain, Limbourg sits uncomfortably close to the German border. This is where the author's Belgian grandmother grew up as a child. In this town there is a war memorial which is instructive. It commemorates not only the names of local soldiers who were killed in battle but also five or six civilians who resisted the Germans in those early days and another two men deported to Germany as slave labourers.

Faced with this onslaught, many Belgians decided to leave and seek sanctuary and safety. Around 325,000 Belgians crossed the border into France and approximately one million crossed into Holland. At the same time, 250,000 Belgian refugees took to boats crossing the English Channel to Britain.[2]

The Germans had violated a treaty initiated by Britain seventy years earlier. With tales of atrocities emanating from Belgium, sympathy in Britain for the plight of these people was overwhelming. It should be said that many newspapers did 'over-egg the pudding' by printing quite lurid accounts of atrocities. These included the infamous 'bayoneting of babies' by German soldiers and displaying them on their shields. There is, of course, no evidence to support this and thus such 'accounts' must be viewed as an extreme form of anti-German propaganda. The reality as already described, however, was enough to ensure horror and sympathy in equal measure and an early welcome for the Belgians arriving in Britain.

In the very early days of the war, the Belgians were able to feel safe in the port city of Antwerp to which many had fled. However, the German troops advanced rapidly, so that by early October they had reached the town. As their army advanced, 1 million residents evacuated the city in one day. By the time the city fell on 10 October it was deserted, and a mere five days later Ostend fell. All of this swelled the number of refugees fleeing to Britain.

The government had tasked the Local Government Board (LGB) with the responsibility for refugee war relief. At the ports they mounted posters proclaiming:

Big welcome in England. You will go to London.
Everything will be arranged for you.
Vive La Belgique![3]

When the arrival of the refugees started, the LGB sprang into action organising the reception at the ports and accommodation for tired and bewildered refugees.

The War Refugees Committee (WRC) was established and based centrally at the General Buildings in the Aldwych, London. Interestingly, one of its organisers was a certain Herbert Gladstone, son of the Victorian prime minister of that name.

In parallel, a War Relief Fund had been set up in August. It was intended initially to aid the indigenous population but as the economy was in better shape than expected it was able to help with the WRC and the many sub-committees that spawned from it. On 24 August, just ten days after the declaration of war, a public appeal resulted in offers and donations from individuals and institutions that would allow the committee to provide hospitality for 100,000 refugees within 14 days. This kind of response was unprecedented and reflected the public support for the refugees.

The LGB ran a well-organised operation in concert with the WRC. They met the refugees at the ports and tended to initial needs, such as clothing and worn-out shoes. The WRC was closed on Saturday but lists of hospitals with accommodation was to be provided at once to the LGB. In turn, the LGB would give WRC notice of the arrival of refugee trains to London and other destinations.

Horrified at the plight of the Belgians, people rushed to help and form sub-committees of the WRC to organise the necessary assistance. The committees were overwhelmingly run by middle-class ladies with time to spare, and a bevy of servants to support them. We are taught that during this war the suffragettes gave up their campaigning to help the war effort. In at least one case it was specifically to help the refugees. For example, in Ealing the London Society for Women's Suffrage suspended their activities when they helped establish the Castlebar Hostel.[4]

The numbers sound overwhelming and indeed never before had such a sudden influx of refugees to this country happened. However, it is salutary to recognise that the situation was helped by the fact that plans had been developed and instigated before the outbreak of war. In fact, emergency contingency planning had been developed to cope with a feared influx of Protestant refugees from Ireland in the event of civil war arising there. This provided the bedrock for planning when the Belgian refugee crisis occurred.

Accommodation needed to be sourced both in London and across the country, which of course included Ireland, part of Great Britain at that time. Large public buildings were requisitioned, which included the exhibition sites of Earl's Court and Alexandra Palace.[5] Photographs show hundreds of beds laid out side by side to cope with the numbers. The wonderful Belgian genealogist, Marie Cappart, personally informed the author that when she was a child her grandmother had advised her that in the event of a war she should 'go to Earl's Court where they would be able to help her'. Such a folk memory is testimony to the tremendous feeling that Belgians had for the support offered them in that war.

At these venues, the refugees would be offered medical checks and clothes, if needed. Conditions were basic, and at the beginning people were sleeping on coats.

During the whole period of the war, 100,000 refugees stayed at Earl's Court and 500 people a week at Alexander Palace.

It was also agreed that workhouses could be used as a temporary measure with various provisos: that the government should pay the bare costs; refugees should be kept separate from ordinary residents; there should be no charge on the Poor Rate and the Local Government Board would pay up to 10 per cent per person.

Refugees were accommodated at Endell Street in Holborn; the Strand Union; Millfield House at Edmonton; Bermondsey; Loughborough and elsewhere.

It was deemed necessary to move the refugees on as soon as possible since so many people were crowded into the two huge exhibition centres. This is where the sub-committees organising local help and accommodation came into their own.

The enthusiasm of the population to look after the Belgian refugees was overwhelming, demonstrated by the 2,500 sub-committees that were established. Throughout the nation, in the many London boroughs, and other large cities such as Birmingham, Manchester and Glasgow, people rallied around to help these Belgian refugees at their darkest hour.

The counties and rural areas were equally supportive. In many ways in those early days, 'assisting the poor Belgians' was very much viewed as part of the war effort. 'Our boys' were going off to fight the Germans and on the home front people wanted to do as much to help those refugees so sorely wronged by the enemy.

Lady Lugard (née Flora Shaw), by profession a journalist, who was prominent in the founding of the National War Refugees Committee, gave full voice to a strong collective feeling: writing in 1915 she said, 'Belgium bore for a time the burden of the world and the world can never forget or repay.'

Information concerning the work of some sub-committees was available in local archives. However, following the commemoration of the First World War, local history societies have undertaken much more research, which is now available online and provides a rich picture of the refugee support activity undertaken.

Within London there were a number of projects which were organised to secure employment for refugees. At the Anglo-Belgian Lace Hostel in Upper Brook Street, Mayfair, a home was provided for refugees and the opportunity to make the lace products they had undertaken at home. The managers countered any charge that they were in competition with home-grown lacemakers since the products were only sold at the hostel.[6]

Wimbledon in London was probably one of the more high-class refugee committees. It was instigated by the journalist Richardson Evans together with Princess Henrietta, who was the sister of King Albert of the Belgians. As early as 17 October 1914, a ceremony which hosted 100,000 people, was held on Wimbledon Common to welcome the Belgians.

In total, 473 refugees were helped there. Two large hostels in Raynes Park accommodated many of the refugees, with others being hosted in private houses. Children were admitted to local schools; a Belgian Boy Scouts' group was set up, and sewing and other classes were organised for the women.

In the East End of London the following letter to the *Hackney Gazette* provides an insight into how housing was procured and how it was paid for. There was a recognition that people wish to support refugees but that they needed to be recompensed.

The Hackney Gazette: Monday 1st March 1915
'Hospitality for Belgian Refugees'

Correspondence to the editor,

'Sir – it is probably not unknown to your readers that, through the activity and kindness of local residents, hospitality is being given in Hackney to a number of Belgian refugees.

There is great need for further assistance of this character, owing to the constant arrival of additional distressed persons from Belgium, and the Belgian Refugee Committee for Hackney, have undertaken, in common with similar bodies throughout the kingdom to take charge of and find homes for a number of these refugees.

The persons for whom the Hackney Committee have undertaken to find residential accommodation are single men of commercial and professional classes. I should be most grateful if any of your readers who would take one or more of each refugees into their homes on boarding terms would communicate with me at once. I particularly address this appeal to local residents who, while anxious to assist the gallant and self-sacrificing Belgian nation in its hour of need, are not in a pecuniary position which would permit of free hospitality being given. My Committee will make arrangements to secure that those who are kind enough to respond to this appeal shall not suffer any financial loss by so doing, as the out-of-pocket expense of the maintenance of the refugees will be defrayed by the Committee. Those, however, who give hospitality to such persons will have the satisfaction of knowing that by offering their homes for the purpose mentioned, and by the service they are thus rendering, they will be doing all that lies in their power to promote the object in view, viz. the relief and assistance of the distressed members of the valiant Belgian nation.'

This willingness to support Belgian refugees was profound in the early years of the war. A letter to the committee from Chorley in Lancashire stated: 'We should be glad to offer a home for an Antwerp family. We would have liked to have had some refugees to look after.'[7]

The Edwardian attitudes to class were very much apparent through the War Refugee Committee (WRC) who actively asked for accommodation for better-class refugees, which would separate them from those refugees considered lower class. The Anglo-Belgian Lace Hostel in Mayfair would have been one such to accommodate 'higher-class' refugees.

Hampshire House, in West London, had a Refugee, Housing and Workshops Committee. It included both Belgian and English men and cabinet-making skills were taught.

As the nation's second city, Birmingham took 5,000 refugees.[8] Trains arriving at New Street off-loaded refugees into charabancs, where they were roundly applauded by well-wishers. Birmingham's committee activities centred around 44 Islington Row, which was used as a temporary centre and hostel. A team of volunteers was enlisted to help process the new arrivals.

Trainloads of refugees would arrive in the city with little or no warning and it was down to the planning and organisational skills of those involved in the Refugee Committee that people were helped and integrated into the daily life of the city. The WRC's role was to help the refugees with housing, employment, education and entertainment. Several sub-committees were founded to deal with these matters. The priority was to find accommodation for the refugees. This process was helped by generous offers from the public. The committee organised English lessons for adults, founded a 'Belgian School', raised funds to maintain destitute Belgian families, helped families to be self-supportive and provided opportunities for employment. They also established a Lost Relatives Bureau, a Belgian club, *Le Cercle Belge* and a maternity home. Material help was offered by the distribution of donated clothing, boots and other gifts.

The chocolate makers Cadbury were Quakers and pacifists but looking after the refugees was an activity they could undertake willingly. Elizabeth Cadbury, wife of the company's chairman, was on the executive committee and ran the allocations committee. They interviewed newly arrived families, assessed their needs and placed them accordingly in accommodation. Many went to private houses and others to large properties that had been converted into hostels. Moor Green House in Moseley was one such place and is now the headquarters of the Church of Scientology in Birmingham.

Among the many committees that were set up was the Birmingham Citizens' Committee, of which the following were branches: the Moseley Auxiliary Branch and the Belgian Refugees Home Committee, Ladies Section.

Many refugees were not barred from remunerative work; a situation very different from today where those claiming asylum have to wait until their claim is granted before they can undertake paid employment. Records show that many of these people found employment at the Austin car plant at Longbridge. The factory had been converted into the production of war work at the time, and was producing lorries, planes, armoured vehicles and munitions throughout the war's duration.

The factory's workforce expanded from 2,500 employees in 1914 to a peak of 22,000 in 1917, so the refugees would have been a welcome addition to the company's human resources, particularly as there were quite a few who had experience of working in the munitions industry at home. Another industry where previous experience proved useful was the jewellery trade. Other companies, such as Cadbury, played their part too, although the Cadbury family were far more directly involved in the welfare of the people than in the production line.

When the war ended in 1918, most refugees returned home. A farewell gathering was arranged and people congregated in the town hall to say their goodbyes and offer thanks for the hospitality of the people of Birmingham. A plaque was presented to the lord mayor as a token of the refugees' thanks and, to this day, it can be seen inside one of the entrances to the Council House.

Many of the refugees made friendships with local people which remained for life. One example was discovered by a Birmingham archivist during the preparations for the hundredth anniversary of the arrival of Belgian refugees. A Belgian refugee called Yvonne had continued to visit neighbours and friends she had made in King's Norton during the First World War up until the 1960s.

Devon and Cornwall Refugee Committee

This committee had its first inaugural meeting on 25 September 1914. The committee members elected were the mayoress who became president; Lady Fortescue, vice president; Miss Andrew, honorary secretary and Mrs Worthington, assistant honorary secretary.[9] Their first task was to make an appeal for funds and they raised £450 within two weeks. To complement this, many homes and vacant houses were offered. The places were agreed and it was on this authority that Miss Andrew travelled to London and returned with 120 refugees. Records at the Devon Heritage Centre show that Exeter was the first provincial city to receive refugees and to provide them with homes. By the end of October, over 800 refugees had been accommodated in the neighbourhood and by the following February the number had grown to 3,000.

By now the task was expanding so much that the lord lieutenant of the county was asked to organise a wider committee which amalgamated Devon and Cornwall and which could provide the scope to disperse people over a wider area.

To aid their work, the Dental Hospital, at 24, Southernhay, was loaned to the committee as a headquarters, free of charge. Their offices were open Monday to Saturday from 10am until 5pm.

There was a large volume of work with up to fifty letters a day. Between the team of volunteers they could interview up to 100 people within twenty-four hours. On one notable occasion a telegram arrived at 10pm, stating that 100 people were being sent to arrive by train at 2.15am the following day. As it transpired, 235 refugees actually arrived and all were housed. Two or three hundred people might come by night; on arrival they would be met by trams and taken to one of the hostels. In total, 8,000 refugees came to Exeter and were dispersed throughout Devon.

In 1916, the government took over the responsibility for grant-funding the work, on the understanding that it would be supplemented by local donations. When work was at full steam, disbursements totalled £2,000 each month.

In Devon, the class attitude to refugees was reflected again – such as when it was recorded: 'there was tremendous generosity; sometimes they were not very desirable visitors and more often were persons with a different standard of living and observance to those who housed them'.

With the expansion of the work of the War Refugee Committee, sub-committees were established across the county. There were, for example, a number of refugees accommodated in Teignmouth, South Devon which in current times houses a rather splendid memorial, a decorated urn, in the gardens near the seafront, thanking the local inhabitants for all the support they gave to the Belgian refugees. It was noted that employees of the Steam Laundry contributed 5s a week to the Belgian Relief Fund. That was not an inconsiderable sum for working people in those days.

Teignmouth's neighbouring town, Shaldon, was hosting 324 refugees in April 1915 at the cost of £594 5s.

The refugees who came to stay in Tavistock, West Devon, had a plaque placed in the guildhall, expressing their gratitude to the people of the town for their warm welcome and hospitality.

Other towns who hosted the refugees were Torquay, Newton Abbot, Bideford and Barnstaple. Plymouth itself was a prohibited town because of naval security but they had been able to arrange for a small number of places via the police on special recommendation. Just outside Plymouth, Lord Seaton was hosting Belgian refugees in his large house at Beechwood. It was noted that despite restriction on hosting, Plymouth had contributed more to the relief fund than anywhere else in the county.

In Cornwall, refugees were accommodated at Launceston, Bude, Port Isaac and Polzeath. The story of an artist from Bruges in St Ives is recounted below.

Louis Reckelbus (1864–1950): a Belgian refugee art teacher[10]

Reckelbus was among the first of ninety-nine Belgian refugees to be settled in St Ives, one of the first towns in Cornwall to welcome refugees from that war-torn country. And it was the women artists who played a major role in organising and promoting the relief to finance the Belgians' stay over the next few years.

Largely self-taught, Reckelbus came from the city of Bruges, and soon played a major part in the life of the St Ives' community. He helped to raise significant sums of money for his compatriots by selling his paintings through the Belgian Refugees Fund Committee, of which he was an active member. There is a fine example of his work which depicts fishing boats off Godrevy, which was exhibited at the Penlee House Gallery and Museum in Penzance in 2010 at their exhibition *Sea Change – Art in St Ives 1914–1930*.

Reckelbus also offered painting lessons. One of his students was Frances Lloyd, the daughter of a prominent American painter, who moved to Bridge Cottage at Zennor. She was the grandmother of the composer George Lloyd, who was born at the St Eia Hotel in St Ives in 1913. While in the town, Reckelbus used the studio of the photographer and musician Herbert Lanyon, father of painter Peter Lanyon.

On his return to Belgium at the end of the war, Reckelbus kept in contact with events in St Ives by taking the local paper, *The St Ives Times*. He said: 'I always think of my exile which I always associate with a little unspoiled Paradise … inhabited by a noble and generous people to whom no form of suffering appeals in vain'.

As soon as the war started and the plight of the Belgian refugees became known, Scotland stepped up and received refugees willingly, such is the generosity of Scottish peoples to people in such plight. The largest number, around 20,000, went to Glasgow but many moved on.

In October 1914, the *Perthshire Advertiser* stated that a furnished cottage for seven refugees had been offered by Mr Hamilton-Smith of Almondbank.

In Methven, just west of Perth, a terraced group of houses were granted to refugees. The *Perthshire Advertiser* wrote about the refugees walking round and enjoying themselves 'making normal their acceptance into the community'. Sixty-three refugees were brought to Crieff and housed in what was previously a homeless hostel. Then in Pitlochry, the provost, together with ladies and gentlemen of the area, welcomed the refugees.

In 1914, Ireland was still a part of Great Britain so that when refugees were arriving in large numbers in the south and east of the country it was decided to send some to Ireland. Workhouses were opened up in Dublin and Dunshaughlin, the latter having already been rejected by the military because the facilities were in such poor condition. Living there took its toll; several refugees died and without access to any resources were interred in paupers' graves.

The refugees who were dispersed to the town of Monaghan fared rather better; houses were found for them in the centre of town in a building still dubbed Belgian Square and it was from there that refugees started an embroidery business. This grew into the Bellbroid Lingerie factory, which by 1923 employed 180 local people.

There was a pre-existing link which brought Belgian refugees to live in Monaghan. Mrs Helen Fowle was a member of a small Belgian-Irish community in the area. She spoke Flemish, which was a real bonus since it was barely spoken in either England or Ireland. She was responsible for bringing Belgian refugees to the area and this knowledge and connection ensured that she was elected chair of the committee.

Plans were underway to bring more people over to Ireland in order to relieve the pressure on services, when tragedy struck. On 26 October 1914, a ship, the *Amiral Ganteaune*, carrying refugees was torpedoed in the English Channel. News of this attack on a French vessel spread fear and panic and ensured it would no longer be viable to ask refugees to make two sea journeys to reach an offer of safety.

The aristocracy within the local area employed refugees as French language tutors. Other skills were harnessed to enhance their social status and that of their families. However, there was a darker side to this. Refugees were being supported under the Poor Law which meant if a person had no resources their only choice was to enter the workhouse.[11] Lady Fingall, a local aristocrat, took it upon herself to select such 'undesirables' at the railway station and drive them to the Dunshaughlin workhouse, mentioned previously as the scene of the Belgian refugee deaths.

Around 100 Benedictine monks from Charleroi in Belgium had been brought to Endermine House in County Wexford to preserve their community. They continued a mission to send monks back to Belgium to act as stretcher bearers for the Belgium army.

In county Galway, Catholic nuns, who had been rescued from a nunnery in Ypres, Belgium, came to live in the beautiful area of Connemara where Kylemore Abbey is now located. Their nunnery had been surrounded for much of the war in Belgium, until they were finally rescued by the 8th Battalion of the Royal Munster Fusiliers. Before they left their nunnery, they secretly hid their religious treasures, which had been accumulated over centuries and included many objects made from gold. At the end of the war, they returned to their original nunnery to find that their treasures had not been discovered and they now possessed much wealth. It was from this source that the order of nuns was able to buy Kylemore Abbey in 1920. It is worth noting that the girls' school that they founded became one of the most prestigious in Ireland.

Education

As there were so many families with children amongst the refugees arriving, there was clearly a need for the provision of education. People tend to think optimistically and as had been experienced in the preceding South African War/Boer War it was believed that 'the war' would be over soon. So organising schools for the children was not seen as a main priority. The children would soon be returning to their country of origin with their families. However, by 1915, the register of refugees that was being drawn up indicated that among the refugees there were 33,000 children between the ages of 5 and 15, who required specific assistance, but it was not until November 1915 that Lady Gladstone established an education department. This work fell under the auspices of the War Refugee Committee once more. And so it was that Edwardian attitudes continued to prevail with class differentiation to the forefront when placing children in schools.

From the outset, children had been placed in local schools as the most practical solution before the department was established but having an education department was considered necessary to regularise matters.

An interesting debate arose in Exmouth over funding for refugees.[12] Two Belgian boys, who were considered bright and able, wished to remain in an educational setting beyond the statutory age of 14. The committee objected, saying that they should not fund these boys above the level that would be paid for local English boys.

A Jewish refugee school was established at Poland Street, Soho for working-class orthodox Jewish children from Antwerp. We have a comprehensive account concerning this school since their day book is in the archives at the London Metropolitan Archives (LMA).[13] The school opened on 9 November 1914 and closed on 27 June 1918 as the pupils had begun returning to Belgium. As a Jewish school they celebrated many religious holidays including the Feast of Weeks, the Jewish Sabbath, Passover, the Day of Tabernacles and the eve of the Day of Atonement. For each of these days the school closed. They also celebrated Empire Day, Belgian Independence Day and Christmas Day. The school roll varied between 200 and 250 pupils.

The school started with a reasonable array of equipment; 40 dual desks, 2 blackboards, 2 easels and 2 tables. Exercise books, pens, crayons and ink were available and reading books had been donated to the school.

The head teacher was Mrs Mayer, who was English, but they also employed two young Belgian women teachers. There is something of a theme whereby there was quite a lot of sickness amongst these teachers but no real explanation is given in the day book. We do not know if the young women, one from Bruges and one from Antwerp were settled in permanent accommodation nor how far they had to travel. Mrs Mayer does record outbreaks of more serious illnesses amongst the pupils, which included scarlet fever and measles. Towards the end of the school's existence, in the summer of 1918, twenty-five fell ill with influenza, which was presumably the virulent strain which erupted in the last months of the Great War and continued into 1919.

There were extra-curricular activities similar to those that took place in all ordinary schools. All the children entertained wounded soldiers. But certain activities seemed to mirror the gender division. In 1915, all boys over the age of ten years were taken to see a matinee at Sadler's Wells, while the girls had laundry and cookery classes. However, in 1917, thirty-eight girls were allowed to swim at Marshall Street baths with only nine boys.

As a school in the centre of London there were additional risks. In June 1917, those very same Germans from whom the refugees had escaped, instigated day time air raids. And on 13 June, thirteen of the girls, following the advice of their parents, refused to go to the cookery and laundry centre because of the air raids.

Across the country, the Belgian children attended school alongside their English contemporaries. The government made money available to support the schools which had admitted refugee children into their classes. It was to an extent similar to the current Pupil Premium measure since it was calculated per head although the head teachers felt it made sense to pool the monies across the school.

Much later in the war they started to create separate Belgian schools with a view to their return home to their country of origin.

Fee-paying schools admitted refugee children as well. Blundell's, a public school near Tiverton in Devon, had the following boys on their roll:

Van der Meersch, Pierre, thirteen and one month and Maurice twelve and four months old, both sons of Eugene and Marguerite Van der Meersch: January 1915 to summer 1916.

Scittekatte, Roger son of Xenophon (engineer in Belgian army) and Melanie. Bridge House, Tiverton.

Van Velsen, Alfred son of Raymond, Master Printer and Julia, Bridge House, Tiverton May 1915 to May 1916.

The mayor of Tiverton accepted a degree of responsibility for trying to find accommodation for two boys who needed to stay in the town over the Christmas period:

Dear Sirs,

I have been asked to find a home for two boys one aged nine years old and one boy aged thirteen years during the Christmas school holidays from December 21st to January 19th. Mother and father are with the Flying Corps of the Belgian army but the boys must stay in England. They speak English well and are excellent companions.

The home must be near Tiverton with some kind-hearted people, fond of boys who would take them for a short period. I shall be grateful for any help. If necessary a small payment can be made for out of pocket expenses.

Very truly yours,
Alfred T. Gregory, Mayor 18th December 1915[14]

Brighton Grammar School

In 1914, Brighton Grammar was a fee-paying boarding school when it accepted five Belgian refugee boys. (At this time all grammar schools were fee-paying.) As with Blundell's, it had admitted boys who had fled the German advance into Belgium. Also joining the school in 1914–15 were seven boys from France, whose families may have wanted them moved out of reach of any potential German incursion.

But three pupils came directly from Antwerp in Belgium after the dramatic fall of that city.

Marcel Tolkowski was 15 when admitted whilst Albert Goldberg and Jacques Votion were only 14. It is worth noting their ages since, after only a year in England, Jacques Votion volunteered for army service; he was the youngest of his peers to do so having claimed on his enlistment to have been born in Surrey in 1896.

Past and Present, Brighton Grammar School magazine, recounts that by November 1916 he was already discharged from the East Surrey Regiment having been wounded at the Battle of Loos. Having fought for the British, Jacques was later to be found working with the 'Church Army huts' in Rhyl. (These were recreational facilities provided by the Church Army for convalescing soldiers.)

Albert Goldberg (by then known as Albert Gould) enlisted into the Royal Fusiliers in 1918.

Munitions

The war was 'hungry' for munitions and Belgians in this country were fully involved in producing them.[15] In October 1914, a French engineer called Pelabon, who had been working in Belgium before the war, arrived here with some of his own workers. He found the ideal spot for a munitions factory on the site of the old roller skating rink by the River Thames at East Twickenham, Richmond. The demand was enormous and soon he was employing 2,000 men. A community of almost 6,000 people was generated in the area and featured its own shops and businesses. It became known as Little Belgium. Pelabon supported at least one school in the area, at Warrington Road, and in 1916 he opened a convalescent home for Belgian soldiers.

After the war, the factory was demolished and an ice-skating rink was built on the site. In the 1960s the author spent happy Saturday mornings ice-skating there without being aware of the connection with Belgian refugees.

At Birtley in the north-east of England another munitions factory was established. It employed injured Belgian soldiers and women. Whilst the community at East Twickenham was totally Belgian, with its own shops and businesses, the one at Birtley went one stage further. It was an enclosed community with its own rules and police force staffed by Belgians.

In 2006, when the author first looked into the stories of Belgian refugees from the First World War, there was some information online and in archives. However, since the hundred-year commemoration of the war information has blossomed. Many local history societies have researched the committee work carried out in their areas to help the refugees. Their accounts paint a graphic picture of life for the refugees and their helpers 100 years ago.

Interest in the period also led to larger projects. The author has been privileged to be given an account of two of these.

As part of a Heritage Lottery Funded bid, the Devon Remembers Heritage Project (DRHP) was established at the Devon Heritage Centre (formerly County Record Office) in late 2014, to commemorate the centenary of the First World War. The project was managed by Katherine Findlay in conjunction with the South-West Heritage Trust. In 2016, Ciaran Stoker joined the project as lead researcher on a number of micro projects looking at life in wartime Devon, including a study of the Belgian refugees in the county.

Ciaran's work included producing multiple chapters in the DRHP's published collection, *Devon During the First World War (2018)*, as well as contributing to a series of interviews with BBC Radio Devon and an exhibition held at the Royal Albert Memorial Museum in late 2018. Additional to this, Ciaran presented his research at a conference held in September 2018 at KU Leuven Campus, Brussels. The conference, titled 'Where do we go from here?' gathered academics from across Europe to discuss their findings on the Belgian refugee experience during the First World War and to agree next steps in this important area of historiography.

Now working for the University of Exeter in a non-research role, Ciaran continues to deliver talks on his research into Belgian refugees in Devon during the First World War to local history groups around Devon and Cornwall. The audiences of Ciaran's talks often know little or nothing about this major chapter in their county's history and are greatly surprised to learn of the volume of Belgians who stayed in Devon. The research enables audiences to draw parallels to refugee crises in the modern world and encourages them to look further into the history of their communities during the First World War. On occasion, history groups provide stories of their own research into the Belgians locally so it is a learning process for the speaker, too. Through the talks, it is hoped people are inspired to explore Devon's past for themselves and engage more with public history institutions like the Devon Heritage Centre.

Wren Music have donated their song *Belgian Refugees* to this publication which was also composed specially for the Devon Remembers Heritage Project. This can be seen in the plate section of the book.

Jeanne Marie Krott

The author did not learn about her late grandmother's history until after her death, nor substantially until after her own mother had died. It was during the process of packing up her belongings at a time when her father was moving into residential care that the author found an autograph book. The keeping of signatures and mementos in such a book was much more common in the early twentieth century. The author's grandmother's autograph book showed its first entry in 1919 whilst she was working as a chambermaid at the Strand Palace Hotel in London. There were signatures, poems and even drawings from her time working at this hotel, from colleagues and also from guests who were staying there. Hotels at that time were often seen as providing long-stay residences and this one in central London entertained guests from a variety of nationalities: Canadians, French and Egyptian. A watercolour of flowers and a pen and ink cartoon reflected the lengthy stay of those guests.

The author had known little about her grandmother but this find inspired her to explore her personal history. Her enquiries soon revealed that 250,000 Belgian refugees had poured into Britain in 1914 when the Germans overran their country. The author wanted to research the history of those frightened people and most particularly uncover her grandmother's part within that significant historical episode.

The author found some general information online and in September 2006, together with her elder son visited the village of Dolhain, Limbourg in Eastern Belgium, which lies very close to the German border. At that time information available was minimal and it is noteworthy that a plethora of local and family history studies have mushroomed since the commemorations for the centenary of the Great War in 2014. The author set out on a quest to trace the movements of her grandmother from Belgium to England.

Civil registration was obligatory in Belgium so painstakingly the author was able to trace her travels from workplace to workplace, which took in a number of towns. From 1908 to 1911 Jeanne-Marie worked variously in Limbourg, Liege, Theux, Verviers and Brussels, always being listed in official documents as a servant or domestic servant.

The author contemporaneously read about other Belgian refugees who came here and found they had been welcomed and that they had spread far and wide across Britain.

At one point the government authorities attempted to create a register of the refugees living in Great Britain. A certain T.T.S. de Jastrzebski of the Journal of the Royal Statistical Society undertook to complete this work. However, the author was informed that this was unlikely to be comprehensive and had probably been destroyed. It wasn't until August 2017 that the author was advised by Simon Fowler, a freelance historian and writer, that certain records of Belgian refugees were being held in the Royal Archives in Brussels. He also suggested making contact with Marie Cappart. It was as a result of these contacts that the author found herself perusing the papers of Jeanne-Marie Krott in March 2018. These original papers showed that she was a Belgian refugee arriving in London in August 1914. Her movements between jobs were recorded meticulously with each hotel being named.

Now her occupation was listed as chambermaid. One paper recorded information about her family and contained the significant fact that her mother had died in 1905.

The author's search had taken her through card indexes at The National Archives at Kew (TNA); hostel lists; a workhouse record on microfiche but all to no avail. However, after eleven years of searching the author was able to see all her grandmother's movements as a refugee in London. These records show that the majority of the refugees returned home in 1918/1919. However, the author's grandmother was one of the estimated 9,000 Belgian refugees who remained.

The author has gleaned her story from her mother and some records. Jeanne-Marie stayed at the Strand Palace and around 1919/1920 formed a relationship with a French man called Marcel leMaire. An inscription in the autograph book showed him writing to the author's grandmother in a romantic old French style. The author's mother was born in March 1921 and it appears they did all go to Paris around 1922, as there is a photo of the author's mother, aged around 15 months, taken in a well-known Parisian photographer's. For reasons the author is unlikely ever to discover, the relationship finished around 1923 and Jeanne-Marie returned to London with her young daughter. She continued work at the Strand Palace Hotel until she died in 1946. In the early years she placed the author's mother with different foster parents during the week, religiously taking her out each weekend. By the time the author's mother was 15 years old they rented a flat together near Oxford Street and lived happily there until the author's mother was called up to join the Auxiliary Territorial Service (the ATS, the women's branch of the British Army).

The author's mother often referred to the fact that her own mother came from Belgium but never once made any comment to indicate that she was aware that Jeanne Marie was one of the 250,000 refugees who fled from the advancing Germans.

Chapter 8

The Basque Refugee Children

It is generally agreed that Spain had entered the twentieth century as one of the most backward countries in Europe. An aged, decrepit monarchy ruled the country, propped up by the twin pillars of the Catholic Church and an aristocratic officer corps. Following the Great Depression of 1929, Spain fell into an economic crisis resulting in widespread anger and discontent. Eventually, in 1930, the military ruler and leader of the dictatorship in Spain, General Primo de Rivera, resigned and King Alfonso XIII called for democratic elections, ushering in the Second Republic. The election eventually was held in April 1931 and saw Republicans triumph in all the major cities. However, from the outset there were significant issues with Catalonia and the Basque Country who wanted their own independence.

The Republicans wanted to abolish privilege but this was opposed implacably by the military, industrialists, landowners and the Catholic Church. Within the Republican ranks, however, deep cracks were beginning to open and they began to lose support from the industrial working class, as wages fell and unemployment rose.

The events of the two turbulent years in Spain from 1931 to 1933 and the various political interpretations of the period is beyond the scope of this book, although well documented. What is salient is that further elections were held in November 1933 and the results saw right-wing parties triumph with an overwhelming victory. As a consequence progressive legislation began to be dismantled and the result ushered in what became known as *El Bienio Negro*, the two black years.

The communists, socialists, anarchists and trade union activists decided to come together to form the Popular Front.

Again in 1936, further elections were held and this time the Popular Front won. The assassination of a prominent far right-wing leader, Jose Calvo Sotelo, by Popular Front government security forces paved the way for high-ranking military officers, allied to Franco, to organise themselves ready for action. A military coup was instigated in Spanish Morocco and General Franco issued his manifesto from Tenerife, his base in the Canary Islands. Declaring himself head of the army, he moved onto the mainland and the war began.

The war occurred in the context of a Europe bitterly divided and with fascist Italy and Nazi Germany giving support to Franco's Nationalists. This was despite Britain and France drawing up a non-intervention agreement which included Germany, Italy, Portugal and the Soviet Union. The purpose of the non-intervention agreement was to ensure that no other country interfered nor gave military aid to either side in this Spanish Civil War.

It was a severe breach of this agreement which would lead to the flight of Basque children refugees. Franco's nationalist forces were keen to put down the Basque region; despising their radicalism and their fight for autonomy. The ports were blockaded and on 26 April 1937, with the help of Nazi German planes, they undertook the most destructive bombing of the town of Guernica. It was timed to take place on a market day when the nationalists knew the town would be crowded. (In the 1990s similar callous action was taken in the Balkans War when the Serbs bombed the busy marketplace in Sarajevo.) The lives lost and destruction of buildings of Guernica was horrendous. That utter devastation has been forever immortalised in the painting of that name by Pablo Picasso.

The National Joint Committee for Spanish Relief (NJCSR) had been formed in Britain in 1936.[1] It sought to support and protect adult and children civilians on the Republican side. The committee had worked with much vigour and resolve to persuade the British government to offer shelter to the refugees. The government eventually agreed to so but only if the committee agreed to be self-supporting through voluntary and charitable donations. At the end of April 1937, Leah Manning, Labour MP and Secretary of the Spanish Medical Aid organisation, travelled to Bilbao at the request of the Basque delegation. From that time on, she campaigned to arrange for a group of Basque child refugees to be accepted. In fear for their children, a group of parents organised for their evacuation. Most were brought to Bilbao from across the Basque region by train. There were tearful scenes on the quayside as on 21 May 1937 as the ship *SS Habana* set sail from Bilbao. The boat had a permitted limit of 400–800 passengers but such was the fear that nearly 4,000 people boarded the ship. This was made up of 3,826 children, 96 teachers, 108 volunteers and 15 priests. For safety, the vessel was accompanied by three British naval ships. The physical conditions for those on board were terrible, given the overcrowding, lack of sanitation and the occurrence of a terrible storm in the Bay of Biscay. Despite that, and to everyone's relief, it docked safely in Southampton two days later.

There had been outrage in Britain at the bombing of Guernica and much sympathy for the victims. However, backed by their role in the non- intervention agreement, the British government, under Stanley Baldwin, Prime Minister, had only agreed to accept the 4,000 children on the basis that no public money at all would be used for their support.

Baldwin did try to suggest that the climate in Britain would be unsuitable for the children, ignorant of the fact that the north coast of Spain possessed a climate as wet as Britain's. (It is today known as 'Green Spain' due to the amount of rainfall.) An umbrella organisation, the Basque Children's Committee, took overall responsibility and initially the children were accommodated in a camp at Stoneham near Southampton. They were accommodated in army tents not directly borrowed from the government but leased from the military and paid for by the various charitable and church groups supporting the young refugees. There was a real enthusiasm to meet and help the young refugees, with local trade unions pooling their resources to prepare the camp infrastructure beforehand. Local people offered to provide food and youth organisations such as the Boy Scouts, Girl Guides and Boys' Brigade all helped the young Basque refugees to settle in. High level support came from the Duchess of Atholl, the Archbishop of Canterbury and the Quaker chocolate makers, Cadbury and Rowntree.

There is no doubt that the children came from highly politicised backgrounds and it was decided that to keep the peace the camp should be divided into sections of Basque nationalists, Socialist, Communist and Anarchist. The children would then paint their suitcases with appropriate logos such as the hammer and sickle.

Quite early on after their arrival, the fall of Bilbao was broadcast to the children over loudspeakers. Many of these refugee children had families still living in Bilbao and the children exhibited great distress at this unexpected news. Some began to run riot, even escaping the camp for a while. Whilst the staff were able to calm the situation eventually, it provided a pretext for certain newspapers to create slurs against the child refugees.

This included such headlines as 'Unruly Mob of Basque Children', 'Reared in Habits of Violence' and 'Basque Children Stampede'. This contrasted sharply with the views of local people and groups, who had helped at the camp and had become acquainted with the children. Such journalese is intended to give a deliberately negative view and to sway people who had no familiarity with the situation.

These headlines had the potential to affect the fundraising efforts for the refugees and organisers sometimes found it necessary to counter the allegations at public meetings. It was agreed to disperse the children to some seventy 'colonies' around the country. These were a mixture of public and private buildings, staffed by volunteers and supported by donations. As the proposed dispersals to colonies around the country began to proceed there was still much sympathy for the children and indeed the cause of the Republicans against Franco.

The Catholic Church eventually agreed to accommodate 1,200 of the refugees who were of that religion. There had initially been some ambivalence, since the Church in Spain was pro-Franco, but they agreed, nevertheless, to accommodate children in various convents and orphanages across the country.

One of the first colonies, which took 450 children, was organised by the Salvation Army at the Clapton Congress Hall in Hackney. The children were welcomed by locals offering donations such as clothes. The building was not particularly suitable and tales recount some of the boys being a little wild and climbing on the roof. When their parents, back home in the Basque country, heard about these shenanigans, they advised that the children should be disciplined. The Salvation Army's solution, in contrast, was to send many of the children to their farm at Hadleigh in Suffolk, where it was felt that some physical labour and fresh air would be of benefit.

Oxfordshire

In Oxfordshire, four colonies were established in the rural areas of Aston, Faringdon, Shipton-under-Wychwood and Thame.[2] In raising support and monies for these, the organisers emphasised the humanitarian and neutral nature of the children. Any overt alliances to different political groups the children talked of from home were underplayed. The vice chairman of the mayor's Spanish Relief Fund spoke to the *Oxford Mail* emphasising that care of the children had neither a political nor religious bias. Thus, the local press presented the children as politically innocent victims of the Civil War. An appeal in the *Chipping Norton Advertiser* the children were described as 'Terror Stricken Beings'.

The management at the Morris Minor Car Factory in Oxford invited the children for an outing to come and have a look around and see how cars were produced. Mr Arthur Exell, a Communist who worked at this factory, was interviewed later and said that he was certain that the management invited the children to visit the plant and have tea simply because they did not seem to have any political bias.

The children were supported by a wide variety of people across the county. Lord Nuffield headed the subscription list with a donation of £5 and Lord Faringdon, a Labour peer, allowed a group of boys to be accommodated on his estate and supplied milk and eggs free of charge. The local fire brigade arranged for a party for the children, and traders from the Oxford covered market donated food at Christmas. Cora Portillo recalled that Mr Tidy of the local bicycle shop donated bikes to the children at Aston.

Churches and religious groups also gave support. Contributions from Bampton and Lew churches were credited in the *Oxford Mail* in October 1938 and in the same paper a letter appeared from the North Oxfordshire committee thanking Woodstock Road Baptist Sunday School for its collection of toys.

The children themselves, both in Oxfordshire and across the country, were involved in fundraising. They put on displays and concerts, dressed in their own traditional dress.

Significant support was provided by the students at Oxford University. Those from the Modern Languages department offered to teach the children English whilst at the same time practising their Spanish. Others acted as interpreters when the children first arrived at Aston in June 1937.

Mention has already been made of Cora Portillo. She was the mother of Michael Portillo, ex-Conservative MP, having acquired her family name by marrying Luis Portillo, a Republican academic who had fled Franco's Spain. During this period of the war she was both teaching the children and staying one night a week at the home playing an active part in the children's care.

The Labour movement gave widespread support to the young refugees both in Oxfordshire and across country. The support came from Labour party branches and the trade unions. The Faringdon branch of the local Labour party entertained boys from a local colony with comedy sketches and music in May 1938. Such activities were designed to act as a morale booster.

Prominent individuals played a part: Mr and Mrs Lower of Oxford City Labour party formed a committee to help with housing.

The North-East and Cumbria Colonies

For child refugees dispersed to colonies in the north-east and Cumbria, funds were raised from a wide variety of sources.[3] Sympathetic owners lent properties in Tynemouth and Hexham, and Lord and Lady Pease lent Hutton Hall to the committee. The old workhouse in Brampton was renovated as the Children's Hostel. Work was undertaken at cost by volunteers including craftsmen and electricians from local factories and Naworth colliery.

Support for three of the hostels was widespread and its sources varied. This ranged from the Left Book Club putting on a film show, the North Shields Methodist Sisterhood performing plays, and groups of teachers and trade unionists would agree to sponsor a particular child by donating a fixed sum weekly. Many donations came in kind from Co-ops and other stores; knitting groups supplied woollens, and there were food donations, many anonymous. Another source, already mentioned, which was used across the colonies, was for the children to perform to audiences, singing and dancing in their national costume. The Brampton colony mounted evenings of entertainment at the Queen's Hall in Carlisle and at the opening of the town playground in Brampton.

Crucial to maintaining the fundraising was the support from the local Labour movement, including the Northumberland and Durham miners' Lodges. In Hexham, owing to its location, there was, however, little, if any, Labour movement support and it is this colony out of the four that closed early in December 1937. The children then had to be dispersed elsewhere.

Whilst the children did not fit the caricature painted by the *Daily Mail* when still in Southampton, there were inevitable problems arising from their experiences. They were living in a foreign country, without their parents who were still in that terrible war zone back home, and in a country where they didn't understand the language or social mores. There were problems with children hoarding food (though this is often evidence of neglect due to poverty), and at Tynemouth, boys were terrified by an artillery display and hid under their beds at the approach of a passing aircraft. Dealing with this as well as the daily round of cooking, cleaning, washing and providing some form of education fell to the small band of older refugees and local volunteers.

Money and resources were not the only problem for these child refugees and their families. As Franco's forces won the Civil War and he ascended to power, he demanded that the children return, actually printing their names in newspapers and publicly calling their parents traitors. This presented a dilemma, particularly for orphaned children, who could be at risk of being forcibly adopted by Franco sympathisers and other children could have been removed to institutions sympathetic to the fascists. The fascists followed the policy of allowing orphaned babies to be permanently adopted by childless couples with fascist sympathies. Now sixty or seventy years later people are trying to ascertain their parentage and search for their siblings. (This is movingly described in C.J. Sansom's *Winter in Madrid*.)

The Midlands' Colonies

In the Midlands, three homes were set up with the aid of donations and the assistance of volunteers.[4] There was Elford Hall just outside Tamworth; Burnaston near Derby and Aldridge Lodge, Walsall. The Labour-run Walsall Corporation agreed that Aldridge Lodge could be adapted to accommodate fifty of the refugee children.

The first meeting of The Walsall Committee for the Relief of Spanish Children was held on 21 June 1937 at The Council House in Walsall. The committee minutes provide an incredible picture into the running of the house. They include expense accounts for foodstuffs, furnishings, medicines and clothing etc. They also include details of the day to day running of the house. Unfortunately, none of the children are named within the minutes.

About two months after their arrival in England, and with the phenomenal assistance of the Co-operative Society, Cadbury and several other benefactors, arrangements were made for fifty of the children to be collected from Southampton. It was agreed that the transport managers of Walsall and Wolverhampton would provide a bus service for this purpose. The minutes detail the type of buses used: two single-decker Walsall corporation buses, driven by Arthur Morrell and Billy Hall. There was one bus for the boys and one bus for the girls and both were destined for Aldridge Lodge. It was reported that the Basque children were fascinated to see a man in a bowler hat, Alderman Whiston, step out of one of the buses to greet them!

In many ways the organisation of the Basque children's support was not dissimilar to that of the Belgian refugees, albeit on a much smaller scale. There was an overarching organisation, with many local committees who raised monies and provided accommodation and support.

The Basque children arrived in Britain at a time of a highly politicised arena. We have seen that newspapers that were more supportive of Franco tried to make political capital out of the children's behaviour. The British government interpreted the non-intervention agreement to mean that these young refugees could receive no support from public funds. This agreement arose since the British government of 1936 did not want to sour relations with Nazi Germany.

Most of the almost 4,000 Basque refugee children eventually returned to Spain. However, 500 who could not return stayed and made their life in Britain.

Today there exists an organisation which commemorates the exodus of Basque children, namely the Basque Children of '37 Association.[5] The Association was set up in November 2002 by Natalia Benjamin and by Manuel Moreno in collaboration with Helvecia Hidalgo, all of whom had been evacuated children. Both Manuel and Natalia had been independently researching the Basque children in Great Britain and were concerned that much archival material was being lost.

By 2006, the association had grown to over 250 members worldwide. In 2016, the association was changed to become a new, unregistered, charity 'BCA'37 UK' with the aim of advancing the education of the public, academics and students on the subject of the exile in 1937 of 4,000 Basque children to the UK during the Spanish Civil War: for example, by giving talks, mounting exhibitions and the erection of memorial plaques.

In recent years the experience of the Basque children has inspired a novel by John Simmons entitled *Spanish Crossings*. It is based on the fact that his parents 'adopted' one of the evacuated boys, Jesus Iguaran Aramburu, who returned to Spain in 1938.

The story of Marina and Carito Rodriguez, two Basque children

Marina and Carito were the two surviving children of Caridad (née Vega) and Eliacim Rodriguez.[6] Three other siblings had sadly died in infancy. Born in Bilbao, their parents had supported the Republican Party during the 1931 elections in Spain. They were Socialists, not Basque Nationalists, and were middle class. Their father was an industrial draughtsman in the dockyard at Bilbao. Their mother, Caridad, ran a private school helping to prepare women for employment, and was to become a representative of the government by 1937.

Following the monstrous bombing of Guernica, the fall of Bilbao was imminent and, like many others, their parents made the heart-wrenching decision to send their children away to safety. The following is an extract from *Hearts of Giants*: celebrating the lives of Marina and Carito Rodriguez at Dartington.

> Years later, the sisters recall hearing a father at the quayside trying to persuade his child to go aboard saying: 'Don't be silly. It'll only be for two or three months and then you'll be back.' They also talked about the awful decision their parents must have made. Marina said: 'I don't think it is so awful when it is so clear that you have to do it.

It probably was very clear to them and they were determined that we should be safe.' But Carito protested: 'Oh but they were so fond of us.' But Marina could only agree: 'Yes, Cari, that's why- if you are so fond of somebody.'

All the clarity with which their parents had seen their duty could not have lessened the pain of execution; their determination to ensure the safety of their children provided no immunity from the sorrow of separation. It was the very cause of it.

These two teenage girls had left Bilbao on the SS *Habana* in May 1937, bound for Britain. When Bilbao fell to Franco's Nationalists in June 1937, the sisters were still at the camp at Stoneham and knew their dream of returning home soon was not to be realised. After the girls arrived in England, their parents had left the Basque country for Barcelona on the Mediterranean coast. Ten months later their father died a broken man: devastated by the destruction of the world he believed in.

The girls, together with sixty-three other Basque children, were moved to the Langham colony near Colchester run by the Peace Pledge Union. There they met Dr Camps who was to be of such influence in their lives. In a similar manner as happened at other camps, the children would put on shows in national costume to raise money. Carito was a great dancer and loved to use this skill in performances.

When the war ended, Franco was confirmed in power. As their mother was by now working for the Republican government in exile in Bordeaux there was no question of the girls returning home to the Basque country. Whilst at Langham, they had been befriended by a civil servant called Percy Grey who had taken them out for strawberry and cream teas; a great memory for the girls. As the colony was closing, Percy Grey offered them a home for three months and from there they went to Nottingham where they started training as nurses.

Neither of the sisters really took to nursing and eventually abandoned this career and embarked on a course of study so they could pass matriculation in the summer. Margarita Camps, who they had met at Langham, had kept in touch and had recently been offered a teaching post at Dartington Hall in Devon. She was impressed by the sisters' determination to learn and was convinced they would do well at the school. It was on her say so that Mr Curry, the headmaster, agreed to their admission to the school.

Dartington was a progressive school, founded in 1925 by Leonard and Dorothy Elmhirst. (It also had the facilities to accept boarders.) It had a particular philosophy and believed in child-centred education and in its practice broke down the barriers between teacher and pupil by inviting the children to call their teachers by their first names. Lessons were not to be taught by dictation nor by simply copying from the board.

After some induction, Marina became a biology teacher and Carito taught in the junior school. Biology often involved walking down to the River Dart and studying the water creatures such as sticklebacks and caddis fly larvae, which lived in their stone and stick houses sparkling under the water.

Their arrival at Dartington was like a force of nature. Both seemed to be forever dancing and Carito capped that by dancing on the table with clogs on! The open nature of the education and the beautiful setting by the river was much appreciated. Marina wrote that their parents' dream in Spain had been on the side of freedom and trust and that by a stroke of good fortune they had found this in Devon.

After the Second World War had finally ended, the sisters were able to meet up with their mother, Caridad. In Paris she was initially working for the Republican Party and then for UNESCO. A feature of refugees' life is often being separated from loved ones because of war and occupation. And it was no exception for Marina and Carito, who had been unable to see their mother through the long years of the Spanish Civil War and after France was occupied by the Nazis. However, in 1954 Marina was offered a job in Madrid, so she left Dartington to move there. At the same time, her mother left UNESCO and moved to Madrid so they could be together.

Unfortunately, living in Spain did not prove as successful as they had both hoped. The war had ended but Franco and his junta still remained in power in Spain and they did not feel comfortable living in that environment. So it was that Marina and her mother returned to Dartington. They had heard about some houses in Leechwell Lane that were due to be demolished and decided to save them from destruction by buying them. Once renovated and rehabilitated, Marina and Carito and their mother moved into Number One, Leechwell Lane. Gradually they sold the other houses to friends. Percy Grey, their old friend who had helped them following their stay at Langham, came to stay. He had been diagnosed with cancer and they undertook his care, their house becoming a hospice until the end of his life.

Marina was in need of employment upon her return. There were no vacant posts for teachers but she was offered the job of housemother at Dartington Hall School. She had enjoyed teaching and this would not have been her first choice but she accepted it. She fitted the role well and drew praise and warmth from both fellow staff and students.

A change of head teacher in 1969 led to a change in educational philosophy. Royston Lambert pushed for an ethos of *laissez-faire*, where pupils could proclaim their rights without reference to others. The co-operative communal ethos was replaced by an upgrading of the competitive lifestyle. To Marina and Carito this was the antipathy of the values they had brought from Spain and those which Dartington had espoused, and they were not happy with these changes.

In 1975 General Franco eventually died. The sisters rejoiced in their own ways – Marina was so happy that she drank a bottle of champagne she had been saving at breakfast and the pupils were delighted to witness her drunk in celebration! Carito's actions were more subtle. She had always kept a postage stamp with Franco's face in her shoe, so she was stamping on his face as she walked. Upon his death she took it out of her shoe, crumpled it up and threw it away. At last the leader of the regime who had forced them and many other young Basques to flee their homes was dead. The sense of liberation was palpable.

Carito stopped teaching at the junior school in 1980 followed by Marina three years later. On their visits to Spain, they had bought a cottage in Alicante on the Mediterranean Coast, so tended to spend their time between Totnes in the winter and Alicante in the summer. Friends were always invited to stay with them at their homes, since they were very sociable and loved eating and drinking. Basque red meat with a good Rioja wine and whisky late at night were their favourites. Their politics hadn't changed. They were left-wing and agnostic and were horrified when Margaret Thatcher became prime minister. They still reached out to individuals in trouble and in those years visited a Spanish prisoner in a local prison.

Carito died in 2007, followed by her sister, Marina, ten years later. As a sign of how well regarded she was, Marina had an organised group of local carers helping her in her final years.

At Marina's funeral, Michael and Lola Williams said, 'Marina and Carito in their lives more than repaid the help they received as refugees by devoting their lives to helping and inspiring so many by their work at Dartington.'

Their story has been encapsulated in a book called *Hearts of Giants*, collated by John Paige, a retired teacher from Dartington for a commemorative weekend in April 2018 which celebrated the lives and times of the sisters.

Chapter 9

The Nazis and Their Persecution of the Jewish Peoples

I n 1905, the Aliens Act was introduced by a Conservative government. This was the direct result of sustained anti-Jewish agitation. It was the first ever Act requiring immigration officers to question incomers at ports and empowering them to refuse entry for specified reasons.[1] Effectively it targeted poor immigrants, since only those arriving in steerage could be questioned about their ability to support themselves. As a basis for immigration control this theme has continued even to the present day. The 'mad, diseased or criminal' were also to be excluded. Within the act there was a limited provision for people claiming asylum, in that the poverty test was not to be applied for those fleeing war and persecution. It allowed entry for those seeking sanctuary 'solely to avoid prosecution or punishment on religious or political grounds' or for an offence of a political character or persecution involving danger of imprisonment; those at risk of danger to life or limb on account of religious belief. But it is important to note that racial persecution was not included in the Act's definitions.

In both 1914 and 1919, the Aliens Restriction Acts greatly extended powers against incomers. The right of appeal was abolished and the exemption from a poverty test for refugees was likewise rescinded. From that point onwards, refugees had no legal shield save the discretion the Home Office held to grant asylum if the case was deemed to merit it.

Hitler's rise to power began in 1920. In January 1933, he was made Chancellor of Germany and with the passing of the Enabling Act in March 1933 he virtually secured dictatorial powers. His anti-Semitic views were heralded in his autobiographical manifesto *Mein Kampf*.

In 1933, the Nazis began to put into practice their racial ideology. The Nazis believed that the Germans were 'racially superior' and that there was a struggle for survival between them and inferior races. They saw

Jews, Roma (Gypsies), and people with disabilities as a serious biological threat to the purity of the 'German (Aryan) Race,' their so-called 'master race'. The Nazis began a process of persecution of Jewish and other groups. Hitler's legislative powers in the Bundestag were ably reinforced by the SA, his *Sturmabteilung* (Stormtroopers, also known as Brown Shirts), on the streets.

Education and academics were amongst the first targets. Jewish academics in Britain, as a response, formed the Academic Assistance Council, which met for the first time in May 1933.[2] They were shown the declaration which people in Germany had to sign as to whether their parents or grandparents were Aryan. This demonstrated how dangerous it had become for academics there. The thrust behind the meeting was to try to help fellow academics in Germany by finding them posts in Britain or other European countries.

In 1920, following the end of the First World War, some academics had put their names to letters requesting the resumption of cultural relations with Germany. The meeting of the Academic Assistance Council requested that people now put their names to a letter protesting contemporary persecution, which included the mass sackings of Jewish academics. Sadly, the British Medical Association refused to 'publish anything of the sort'. However, it fell to Thomas, later Lord, Horder, a physician at St Bartholomew's Hospital in London (who made his reputation by correctly diagnosing a complaint of King Edward VII), to use his influence with the medical profession in order to make public the protest.

These meetings continued throughout the period until November 1934; their chief object being to find posts for German Jewish academics deprived of their living by the Nazis.

Jewish organisations in Britain had agreed with the government that they would support the refugees financially as a condition of their entry.

Most of the places offered were for scientific posts, although one was available at the London School of Economics. Some were salaried, others were not. For example, the post of Professor of Paediatrics at the Children's Hospital in Birmingham was offered to a German refugee on the basis of providing board and lodging, but without a salary. Knowing what was happening in Nazi Germany made these offers of work literally a lifeline for many academics.

Through personal contacts, a number of posts offered to German Jewish academics were in Belgium, Holland and France, and some were in Palestine.

Those sent to the first-named countries would have had to flee a second time when Nazi troops invaded.

Ultimately 186 visas were issued for professionals, of which most were academics. Sir Henry Pelham of the Board of Education oversaw recruitment of staff from abroad. It was his view that they could not vet German teaching assistants. On the other hand, Sir Lewis Namier, a prominent Jewish professor at the London School of Economics, countered this argument, saying they had to be vetted, on the grounds that the German government would have selected only Nazis to be allowed to come to England. Pelham's kind of British politeness, a little like the refusal of the British Medical Association to speak against the Nazis, was clearly, in retrospect (if not at the time), naïve and showed a lack of understanding of the danger that Hitler's regime now posed.

The last meeting of the Academic Assistance Council recorded was on 15 November 1934.

The Advisory Committee of the Refugee Organisations to the High Commissioner for Refugees from Germany debated the definition of a refugee. Meeting at Woburn House on 15 June 1936, some were worried that if the definition was too narrow it would allow the government to refuse people.

Similarly, people were concerned to design a helpful certificate that would facilitate refugee movement. A suggestion by Mr Battsek, from the Jewish Refugee Committee, was that refugees should be able to speak for themselves. However, Bentwich (representing the Council for German Jewry) said the inter-governmental conference was not there to hear evidence but to reach a conclusion and decide which documents would be required for official identification of individuals.

The chairman wanted to consult with representatives of refugees who would be present in Geneva. From Hitler's accession to power in 1933 almost to the beginning of war in 1939, there were numerous problems since the government either failed to realise the seriousness of the Nazi threat or they didn't want to sour relations with the same German state (the rationale for government thinking at this time is beyond the scope of this book). It should be noted, however, that British people who were Jews working in Germany were not generally defended by the British government if they had been subject to Nazi legislation.

When an employee of Peat Marwick accountants was asked to sign a declaration that his ancestors were Aryan, which he questioned, the Foreign Office decided they could not challenge the German authorities on this matter.

This failure to recognise potential problems and resolve ambivalent attitudes to the growing Nazi threat posed by the German state extended into sport.[4] In December 1935, an international match was due to be played between Britain and Germany at White Hart Lane, the ground of Tottenham Hotspur. This in itself should have raised concerns, since a large majority of Spurs supporters were and are Jewish. Those supporters and anti-fascist friends were concerned that the match would betoken friendship with the Nazis who might be coming to cause trouble at the match. It was planned that leaflets were to be distributed a fortnight before the match by those opposed to Nazi Germany.

The government saw no reason to cancel the match and simply asked that the German government ensure that their supporters remained calm. The German ambassador had undertaken to guarantee the behaviour of their fans. Hitler himself was aware of this particular match and maintained that the decision to cancel should and must lie with the British government, leaving them to be held responsible for any opprobrium and financial costs. Walter Citrine, head of the Trades Union Congress (TUC) took up the cause, thus bringing it to the media's attention. Ultimately, he was mollified by John Simon, the Home Secretary, since he was loath to be accused of bringing politics into sport. In the event the match itself was relatively peaceful with the home side triumphing 3–0. But Jewish people had been persuaded to stay away and as the match began, the German supporters gave 'Heil Hitler' salutes and waved small swastika pennants during the match. That this happened in London at the grounds of a club with a largely Jewish fan-base was a threatening spectacle which could have been avoided.

Shortly after this event, Sir Eric Phipps, British ambassador in Berlin, uncovered a revised Nazi handbook on sport. It advocated anti-Semitic attitudes in sport, distorted facts to conform to the Nazi beliefs and emphasised the political nature of sport. He later said that if the TUC had had access to this book they would have been able to make a stronger case.

The appeasement over the match did little to warm Anglo-German relations. But the effect on Jewish residents here, and those trying to escape to this country, must have been very disheartening.

In 1933, Canada was approached about taking a number of Jewish doctors to work in remote areas but refused this request from the British government. Australia and South Africa were also approached but were equally reluctant. Part of the problem was that, as was common for all these countries, these approaches were being made at a time of high unemployment. New Zealand was more explicit upon being asked, stating that German Jews could have communist sympathies and might stir up trouble.

Well-off Jewish people were loath to support the poorer Jews. As we have seen, there were schemes to help professional people but assistance to other classes were not vigorously pursued.

The Fund for German Jewry was active in pursuing both employment and financial aid in support of saving Jewish professionals. Reading the minutes conveys the sense that this was an organisation which was continually trying to adjust its philanthropic aims to the turbulent political context of pre-war Britain.

Their records provide evidence of the range of financial support provided for refugees:

- A Dr Kurt, who was now working hard for his degree and had a wife and two children to support, was awarded an extra £30 in grant.[5]
- Dr Max Schimtoff was currently working as pupil to a prominent member of the bar was awarded £20 to ensure he spoke perfect English.
- A Czech refugee committee was formed since 85 per cent of Czech refugees were Jewish.
- Five hundred pounds was donated for a children's hostel in Glasgow.

A further minute discusses the members' concern that work permits for domestic servants, which had been issued by the Ministry of Labour, were now to be issued through the Domestic Bureau, which could charge monies for such permits.

There was still an emphasis on trying to find Jewish peoples a safe haven. And it was in this context that £28,000 was awarded to *Keren Hayesod*, an organisation focused on promoting and assisting Jewish people re-settling in Palestine.

However, during 1938 and 1939 both the government and the Fund for German Jewry explored other venues beyond Britain. The possibility of Ireland was not thought likely, although some individual help was possible. Belfast held out the possibility of one or two business projects.

Much further afield, an offer was made of work to ten German Jewish families in the Murranbridge Irrigation area. The Australian Welfare Board costed the project at £16,000 and said they were willing to share the cost with the Council for German Jewry.

The government's Cabinet Committee on Aliens Restriction first met with the British Board of Deputies to negotiate various matters on 6 April 1933.[6] The premise was that if the Board could support people financially then the Cabinet Committee would agree to allow Jewish refugees to enter Britain. It was argued that most refugees would subsequently transmigrate to colonies and elsewhere but on that basis they wanted all German Jews admitted unreservedly. It was still hoped that these admissions would be temporary as settlement was a long-term commitment.

There were specific problems for Polish Jews in Germany. The Nazis persecuted them with particular venom. In 1933, the British authorities withheld visas from them, arguing that they could go back to their own country. Rather than looking at the persecution suffered, the British government chose to look at a seemingly pragmatic solution that the Polish Jews had a country to return to, unlike their similarly persecuted German Jews. We will see a little later that this transformed into a perilous situation.

One problem which cropped up was that Jewish people arriving in Britain often declared themselves as visitors, not being aware that this could cause them problems if they stayed. This is not uncommon when people are uncertain about the future and do not envisage themselves as staying for a lengthy time.

As problems seemingly subsided through 1933 to 1934, some Jewish people decided to return to their homeland. In hindsight this might seem misguided since the Nazis had gained full control of the state machinery, but they had family, work and businesses to attend to and could not foresee how terrible the future would be.

At the same time, British officials thought anti-Jewish feeling in Germany was either not so bad or that it was confined to Germany itself.

There was a strong feeling that Anglo-German relations should not be disturbed and this overarching principle continued throughout the 1930s.

By March 1938, when Hitler's troops marched into Austria to declare 'Anschluss' (Union with Germany), there were many Nazi sympathisers in that country. Crowds lined the streets to welcome the Nazi cavalcade as it rolled into Vienna.

The advent of Nazi German rule was horrendous for Austrian Jews: not only did officialdom persecute them but Nazi neighbours set out to terrorise them, stealing their belongings and trying to harass them from their houses.

In Britain there was shock and sympathy for the way the Austrian Jews were treated but unfortunately practical assistance was limited. From the literature it would nevertheless appear that British Jewish organisations set out to limit how and when they would support Austrian Jewish refugees and the government responded by instigating a system of entry clearance visas. This meant people had to obtain a visa in their own country rather than arriving in Britain and requesting entry.

In Vienna, anxious Jews besieged the embassy, queuing often for days on end. In the climate there this led to harassment from Nazis for whom they were 'sitting ducks'. Being forced to wash cars was one of the lesser indignities. On one occasion members of the SA (Stormtroopers) threatened to enter the embassy and arrest all the Jews waiting. It was only the intervention of the British Consul-General that stopped this.

During 1938, there were increasing demands for the Sudetenland (an area of Czechoslovakia containing mainly people of German origin) to be annexed within the greater German state. It was at this point that Britain and France called for talks with Hitler. In the infamous agreement made in Munich, on 30 September 1938, the British Prime Minister, Neville Chamberlain (as well as the French prime minister), thought he had gained Hitler's agreement that he would not invade any more countries or territories (although agreeing for the Sudetenland to be annexed by Germany). Chamberlain returned to England holding that letter of promise ('peace in our time') as he stood on the steps of his aircraft. This 'promise' was kept until 15 March 1939, when Hitler invaded Czechoslovakia.

With each of Hitler's invasions, the noose tightened for European Jewry and for other of his political opponents.

In the Sudetenland, many Jews were actually refugees from Austria and many had now opted for Czech nationality. The Czech government was aware of this but was loath to accept them. The British government knew this but was not happy to issue visas for these people to come to Britain and seek sanctuary. Instead it offered financial support to the Czech government and offered to assist with emigration to various colonies.

In 1938, Robert Stopford, a banker, was appointed by the British government as the British liaison officer in Prague and was sent there, together with a TUC official, to try and find a way to help the refugees.[7] (Part of his brief was to make sure that there was no discrimination on political or racial grounds.) His mission also collected information on the plight of the Jewish people there; he predicted that 150,000–200,000 Jewish people would soon be forced to emigrate. He alerted Anthony de Rothschild of this imminent catastrophe. Funding was raised but it became apparent that more help was needed than originally envisaged, yet at the same time the British government was loath to spend money.

In Germany, the Nazi regime was intensifying its onslaught on Jewish peoples. Treatment of Polish Jews in Germany has already been mentioned. In addition, the Polish government acted against its nationals returning home. They set up their own guards on the border, blocking entry just as the Nazis rounded up 10,000 Polish Jews and 'dumped' them at the Polish-German border.[8] Prevented from gaining entry to Poland and blocked from returning to Germany these unfortunate peoples were forced to live in inhuman conditions at the Polish border in a place called Zbonszyn. 'Some died and others went mad'. It was many weeks before people were eventually admitted to Poland. But before that happened, a young man called Hershel Grynspan living in France learnt that his parents had been caught up in this awful situation. Distraught

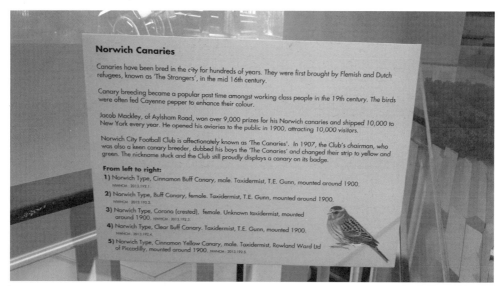

Norwich Canaries

Canaries have been bred in the city for hundreds of years. They were first brought by Flemish and Dutch refugees, known as 'The Strangers', in the mid 16th century.

Canary breeding became a popular past time amongst working class people in the 19th century. The birds were often fed Cayenne pepper to enhance their colour.

Jacob Mackley, of Aylsham Road, won over 9,000 prizes for his Norwich canaries and shipped 10,000 to New York every year. He opened his aviaries to the public in 1900, attracting 10,000 visitors.

Norwich City Football Club is affectionately known as 'The Canaries'. In 1907, the Club's chairman, who was also a keen canary breeder, dubbed his boys the 'The Canaries' and changed their strip to yellow and green. The nickname stuck and the Club still proudly displays a canary on its badge.

From left to right:
1) Norwich Type, Cinnamon Buff Canary, male. Taxidermist, T.E. Gunn, mounted around 1900. NWHCM : 2013.192.1

2) Norwich Type, Buff Canary, female. Taxidermist, T.E. Gunn, mounted around 1900. NWHCM : 2013.192.2

3) Norwich Type, Corona (crested), female. Unknown taxidermist, mounted around 1900. NWHCM : 2013.192.3

4) Norwich Type, Clear Buff Canary. Taxidermist, T.E. Gunn, mounted 1900. NWHCM : 2013.192.4

5) Norwich Type, Cinnamon Yellow Canary, male. Taxidermist, Rowland Ward Ltd of Piccadilly, mounted around 1900. NWHCM : 2013.192.5

The Canaries at the Museum of Norwich at the Bridewell. (*The Museum of Norwich at the Bridewell, 2019*)

Protestants flee Catholic persecution in the 16th and 17th centuries.

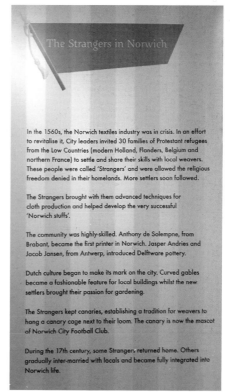

The Strangers in Norwich

In the 1560s, the Norwich textiles industry was in crisis. In an effort to revitalise it, City leaders invited 30 families of Protestant refugees from the Low Countries (modern Holland, Flanders, Belgium and northern France) to settle and share their skills with local weavers. These people were called 'Strangers' and were allowed the religious freedom denied in their homelands. More settlers soon followed.

The Strangers brought with them advanced techniques for cloth production and helped develop the very successful 'Norwich stuffs'.

The community was highly-skilled. Anthony de Solempne, from Brabant, became the first printer in Norwich. Jasper Andries and Jacob Jansen, from Antwerp, introduced Delftware pottery.

Dutch culture began to make its mark on the city. Curved gables became a fashionable feature for local buildings whilst the new settlers brought their passion for gardening.

The Strangers kept canaries, establishing a tradition for weavers to hang a canary cage next to their loom. The canary is now the mascot of Norwich City Football Club.

During the 17th century, some Strangers returned home. Others gradually inter-married with locals and became fully integrated into Norwich life.

The Strangers fleeing persecution in the Low Countries brought many skills to Norwich aiding the expansion of the economy. (*The Museum of Norwich at the Bridewell*)

Fifthly

To the Poor French Refugees in Several Countries of England.

To the Poor French Refugees at Canterbary, for their share of this charity, as appears by the Recit of their Ministers and Elders mark'd N° 1 — £ 180 „ „

To the Poor French Refugees at Exeter for their share of this charity, as appears by the Recit of their Ministers and Elders — N° 2 — 22, 10 „

To the Poor French Refugees at Plymouth for their share of this charity, as appears by the Recit of their Minister and Elder N° 3 — 45 „ „

To the Poor French Refugees at Stone House near Plymouth, for their share of this charity, as appears by the Recit of their Minister and Elders — N° 4 — 28, 16 „

To the Poor French Refugees at Dover for their share of this charity, as appears by the Recit of their Minister and Elder — N° 5 „ 12 „ „

To the Poor French Refugees at La Rye for their share of this charity, as appears by the Recit of their Minister, and Elders — N° 6 „ 27 „ „

£ 315. 6.

Monies paid to poor French refugees c.1697. (*The London Metropolitan Archives*)

Map of Palatine area in the 18th century.

Huguenot church c.17th and 18th centuries, now Brick Lane Mosque. ('*Huguenots of Spitalfields*' *website*)

Belgian refugees flee the advancing German army at the outbreak of World War One, 1914. (*World History Archive*)

Belgians escape on boats, 1914. (*Alan F. Taylor, Folkestone*)

Memorial vase donated to the people of Teignmouth by Belgian refugees. (*Tony Marchese, 2018*)

Jeanne-Marie Krott, the author's grandmother, 26 May 1919. (*Family photo*)

Refugee Song Written for Devon Remembers 2017

Lyrics Marilyn Tucker and Jane Syers
Tune Paul Wilson adapted from Belgian tune
Arr David Faulkner and Paul Wilson

Belgian refugee song. (*Paul Wilson of Wren Music [the musical score and lyrics]*)

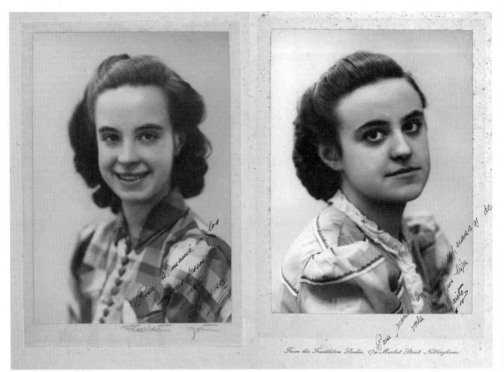

Marina and Carito as young women, c.1940. (*'Hearts of Giants': Image provided by Graham Peet and Dartington archives*)

Carito teaching at Dartington c.1966 (*'Hearts of Giants': Image provided by Graham Peet and Dartington archives*)

Marina and Carito outside their house in Totnes c.2000. (*'Hearts of Giants': Image provided by Graham Peet and Dartington archives*)

Brochure for the unveiling of the plaque to Szmul Zygielbojm, 1996. (*David Rosenberg*)

SZMUL 'ARTUR'
ZYGIELBOJM

1895
1943

*A commemorative brochure
published for the unveiling of
a memorial plaque in London
12 May 1996*

Szmul Zygielbojm memorial plaque in London, 1996.
(*David Rosenberg*)

Surname 1

Other names 2

Place of birth 3

Date of birth 4

Rudi Becker c. 1945. (*Family photo with thanks to Sara Elizabeth Smiles*)

Rudi Becker's photo ID card c.1945. (*Family photo with thanks to Sara Elizabeth Smiles*)

Ilford Park Polish Home, Stover, Devon. (*The Polish Home, Stover, 2019*)

Hungarian refugees at the border, 1956. (*Imagno*)

Plasterdown refugee camp, Dartmoor, 1972. (*Thanks to the Tavistock Museum*)

Bill Meswania outside Veggie Perrins, Plymouth, 2019. (*Tony Marchese*)

Refugees from Vietnam crossing the Perfume River. (*Terry Fincher*)

Vietnamese refugees marooned in Hong Kong, 1978. (*'Vietnam refugees in Hong Kong'*)

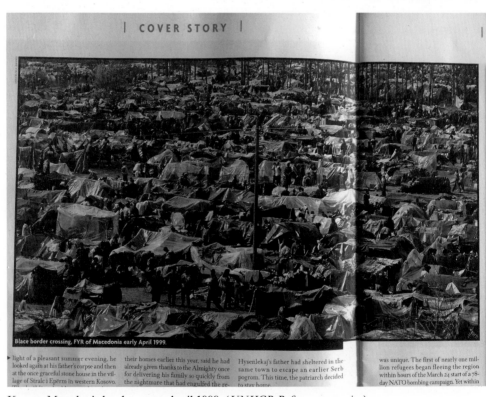

Blace border crossing, FYR of Macedonia early April 1999.

▶ light of a pleasant summer evening, he looked again at his father's corpse and then at the once graceful stone house in the village of Stralc i Epërm in western Kosovo. their homes earlier this year, said he had already given thanks to the Almighty once for delivering his family so quickly from the nightmare that had engulfed the re- Hysenlekaj's father had sheltered in the same town to escape an earlier Serb pogrom. This time, the patriarch decided to stay home. was unique. The first of nearly one million refugees began fleeing the region within hours of the March 24 start of a 78-day NATO bombing campaign. Yet within

Kosovo–Macedonia border camp, April 1999. (*UNHCR Refugees magazine*)

Baki Ejupi who fled from Kosova in 1999, now working as a GP in London. (*Family photo*)

Kosovar refugees' camp in Kukes (Albania), April 1999. (*Dino Fracchia / Alamy Stock Photo*)

Syrienkrieg–Zerstörung. A Ruined house in Idlib, Syria, 2015. (*Adobe stock*)

at his parents' treatment and fearful because his own tenure in France was uncertain, he took a gun into the German Embassy in Paris and shot dead the third secretary.

This sole act resulted in a furious backlash against German Jews. The request by a leading German Jew that non-Jewish officials go to Berlin and try to mediate the resulting crisis was declined. As ever, in Britain it was believed that such an intervention would make the situation even worse.

However, the situation did deteriorate as the event was used as an excuse for the infamous Kristallnacht which occurred throughout Germany on 9–10 November 1938. Thousands of Jewish businesses and homes had their windows smashed and businesses wrecked. After this over 100 Jewish men were killed and 10,000 were taken to concentration camps. Those Jewish people who could prove they had somewhere to go would be freed to go abroad, or so the Nazis announced.

There was horror expressed at home about Kristallnacht but at the highest level of government thinking, attitudes were ambivalent. Neville Chamberlain, in a private letter to his sister, expressed anger and distress about what had happened. However, he also privately thought that the Jews were an unlovable race. Efforts though to help Jews by himself and the Home Secretary, Hoare, were made largely through plans to send Jews to the colonies. Louise London states that a major Jewish organisation in London was involved in admitting individual Jews at the cost of £5,000 which allowed the admission of seventy-five cases daily. They did not want this publicised for fear that some would say it was too many or others that it was not enough, such are the politics of migration numbers.

Despite all previous assurances, on 15 March 1939 Hitler invaded Czechoslovakia, an act which made it crystal clear that he did not intend to keep to any parts of the Munich agreement. Then on 1 September that year the Nazis invaded Poland from the west whilst the Soviet Union invaded from the east, becoming allies on 17 September. The scene was set for the Second World War and the attempted genocide of the Jewish people.

Kindertransport

In response to the horrors of Kristallnacht on November 9 and 10, the British Jewish Refugee Committee appealed to MPs and a debate was held in the House of Commons. The already existing refugee aid committees in Britain switched into high gear, changing focus from emigration to rescue. The British government had just refused to allow 10,000 Jewish children to enter Palestine, but the atrocities in Germany and Austria persuaded most, and the words of British Foreign Minister Samuel Hoare – 'Here is a chance of taking the young generation of a great people, here is a chance of mitigating to some extend the terrible suffering of their parents and their friends' – swayed the government to permit an unspecified number of children under the age of 17 to enter the United Kingdom. It was agreed to admit the children on temporary travel documents, with the idea that they would rejoin their parents when the crisis was over. A £50 bond had to be posted for each child 'to assure their ultimate resettlement'. The children were to travel in sealed trains. The first transport left on December 1, 1938, less than one month after Kristallnacht; the last left on September 1, 1939 – just two days before Great Britain's entry into the war, which marked the end of the programme. The first 196 children arrived at Harwich on 2 December 1938. They were from a Jewish orphanage that had been burnt down by the Nazis on Kristallnacht. Six hundred children arrived on 10 December from Vienna. By the time of the final arrival, some 10,000 children had made the trip.

Kindertransport was the informal name of the rescue operation, a movement in which many organisations and individuals participated.[9] It was unique in that Jews, Quakers, and Christians of many denominations worked together to rescue primarily Jewish children. Many great people rose to the moment: Lola Hahn-Warburg, who set the framework of rescue in 1933 while still in Germany; Lord Baldwin, author of the famous appeal to British conscience; Rebecca Sieff, Sir Wyndham Deeds, Viscount Samuel; Rabbi Solomon Schoenfeld, who saved close to 1,000 Orthodox children; Nicholas Winton, who saved nearly 700 Czech children; Professor Bentwich, organiser of the Dutch escape route; and the Quaker leaders Bertha Bracey and Jean Hoare (cousin of Sir Samuel Hoare), who herself led out a planeload of children from Prague; and many others. Truus Wijsmuller-Meijer was a Dutch Christian who faced down Eichmann in Vienna and brought out 600 children on one train, organised a transport from Riga to Sweden, and helped smuggle a group of children onto the illegal ship *Dora*, bound from Marseilles to Palestine.

Most of these rescuers kept their efforts to themselves. Nicholas Winton's story remained hidden until his wife, Grete, found the scrapbook he had kept with the children's names and photos. Six hundred and sixty-nine children were rescued due to his humanitarian intervention. The story became famous in Britain when, in 1988, Esther Rantzen organised a television programme, which Nicholas Winton attended. During the course of the programme, the audience sitting behind him were asked to stand up if they owed their life to him. They all stood – a most moving piece of reality television.

The Home Service put out a request for foster parents and immediately received 500 offers. It was of note that there was no major inspection of the foster homes nor any requirement that the foster parents were Jewish other than that the house was clean. Recently it was revealed that Clement Attlee, the wartime Labour deputy prime minister in Churchill's government and later Labour prime minister after the war, was one of these foster parents under the Kindertransport scheme.

Foster parents were not available for all children so many were placed in orphanages. Children were spread across the country and were cared for and went to school. But older ones had to conform to British ways and by the age of 14 they were expected to look for work.

In Surrey, three hostels were opened during the period to care for Jewish children. Stoatley Rough School was opened by Dr Hilde Lion, an academic who had left her native Germany when Hitler came to power, and Bertha Bracey, a Quaker who had helped lead children from Prague. Initially they had five pupils but after Hitler's annexation of Austria the numbers rose to eighty-one. A former pupil, Wolfgang Elston, described the school as an oasis of sanity where children could go through all the stresses of growing up, in safety and security.'

The other two places of safety were at Farnham Rowledge Hostel and Weir Courtney House. The latter was founded in 1945 to offer support for those children who survived the Holocaust.

Not all children were young: some were teenagers approaching or having reached school-leaving age. In Gloucester, a home was opened for such boys by GAAR (Gloucester Association for Assisting Refugees). The house had been purchased by GAAR at the cost of £800. It was run by Dr Paul Arnstein and his wife. They were German-speaking and had managed to leave Prague on offer of this job. The house was run as a family home. The boys spoke little English and were sent to the Archdeacon Street School for Boys. When they left school they found various apprenticeships and all went into lodgings found for them by the Arnsteins.

The small town of Llanwrtyd Wells in Wales welcomed 120 of the children.[10] The Czech government in exile rented a large house which would become the Czech Secondary School. When a concert was arranged, the children intended to sing some Slovak and Czech songs but ended up singing *Hen Wlad Fy Nhadau*, the original Welsh version of *Land of My Fathers*, for which the community took them to their hearts. The children were mainly from the group brought out of Czechoslovakia by Sir Nicholas Winton. In later years when his work became public he visited the town of Český Krumlov, from where the children came. After the war, the links between the Kinder and the town continued with personal visits. The town was formally twinned with Český Krumlov in the Czech Republic and a piece of gold was donated for the mayoral chain in Llanwrtyd Wells by the refugees who visited the town.

Occasionally, parents managed to smuggle themselves out of Germany, but the sad truth is that many children never saw their parents again and had to assume, sometimes years later, that they had perished in the Holocaust. A piece of work undertaken by Nicholas Winton's daughter managed to contact 1,000 of these children as adults. Of those, only 50 per cent said that they ever saw their parents again and many had lost entire extended families.

The author worked with a lady in London in the 1980s, who had never discussed much about her family until one day during a social drink in the local pub garden in Greenwich. She revealed that her parents had placed her and her sister on a train in Vienna travelling to London. Just 18 years old at the time, she never saw them again and explained that she avoided looking at any of the pictures of the concentration camps in case she saw her own parents behind the wires. It was a warm summer evening, with the scent of flowers heavy in the air, but the author can still remember the chill she felt hearing these revelations.

Chapter 10

Second World War Refugees in Britain

The period between September 1939 and April 1940 was dubbed the 'Phoney War' in Britain. Expectations of bombing or even land invasion by the Germans failed to materialise. Children had been evacuated from the big cities but many were brought back as it seemed safe to do so.

Things changed when the Germans invaded Belgium, Holland and France. The British Expeditionary Force (BEF), sent to assist the French, had to be evacuated and it was the extraordinary way in which both military and civilian vessels sailing from England achieved this rescue at Dunkirk that has been memorialised down the years. Nevertheless, it shouldn't be forgotten that the BEF lost 68,000 soldiers during their campaign in France.

At home, things changed dramatically when Hitler unleashed his Blitzkrieg on a number of British cities.

Displacement

The Second World War, and the precursor actions of Nazi Germany, which pushed its tentacles across Europe, caused the largest displacement of populations ever witnessed. It has been noted earlier how terrified Jews and other minorities, such as Communists, tried to gain access to this country in the period before the war. By the beginning of the war there were around 10,000 refugees of Jewish origin in the UK. During the war, a further 7,000 gained entry. In Germany itself, as well as the occupied countries of Austria and the Sudetenland, attempting to escape was perilous.

As Hitler's plan to subjugate Europe unfolded, his armies were ordered through countries bordering the North Sea.

Firstly, the Nazis invaded Norway in April 1940. They wanted both the ports that would enable them to control the seas against Britain

and access to Norwegian iron ore, which they could use in their arms'
industry. The Nazis believed that Britain would launch the second front
against Norway. They supplanted the Norwegian flag with a swastika.
Their treatment of Norwegian Jews was cruel as ever, with many being
transported to concentration camps.

Some Norwegians escaped to the Shetland Islands; a perilous journey
in rough seas which had to be undertaken by night with the lights
dimmed. But Shetland was also important in that the British military
trained Norwegians there for missions against the occupying Nazis. The
bravery of the Norwegian village of Telavag is commemorated to this day.
Two trained men shot and killed two Gestapo agents. The Nazi reprisals
were vicious. All adult males were sent to Sachsenhausen concentration
camp where thirty-one died. The women and children were all interned,
and the village destroyed.

The links between Shetland and Norway continue to this day with
certain memorial days being honoured. Links were forged with another
Scottish settlement on the north-east coast of Scotland.[1] Following the
German invasion, hundreds of Norwegian and Danish refugees – men,
women and children – sailed across the North Sea in small fishing boats
to seek refuge in Scotland. Many of these refugees settled in Buckie,
a community of 8,000 people on the Moray Firth coast, and the town
was described as 'Little Norway' during the war years. A Norwegian
Consulate, reading room and *Sjømannskirken* (The Norwegian Church
Abroad) opened in the main street in 1942 and King Haakon VII visited
the town in the summer of 1943. The Danish refugee population,
although smaller, was no less significant a part of the town's wartime
experience and collective memory.

Both the Danish and Norwegian communities were, therefore,
important parts of the life of the town during the war years, bound together
by their common heritage of North Sea fishing and a determination to
achieve victory in the war. Many of these ties have endured ever since.
There were many marriages between Norwegians, Danes and Scots.
Some settled in Scotland permanently, many others returned to Norway
and Denmark with Scottish spouses. Notable figures, such as the
businessmen Trond Mohn and Otto Thoresen, were born in Buckie as
part of this exiled community.

Although the story of the Shetland Bus is well known as perhaps the pre-eminent link between Scotland and Scandinavia during this period, little known is the narrative around the men, women and children from Norway and Denmark who left their homes and found safety in Buckie. It has been recently memorialised in the Buckie and District Heritage Society, which, in collaboration with Professor Reid of the Robert Gordon University Aberdeen, runs a heritage centre telling the history of Buckie.

As Belgium was invaded from the east, a panic took hold of Belgian citizens, no doubt remembering the invasion of the First World War. By 11 May, the roads westward were blocked by fleeing Belgians.

Approximately 15,000 fled their homes. The Belgian military held out against Germans for eighteen days despite overwhelming odds.

But ultimately the Belgian king brokered a ceasefire and surrendered unconditionally. Unfortunately this capitulation led to a somewhat different attitude to Belgian refugees in this war than that afforded them in the First World War.

With the surrender of the Belgian army, the government, led by Hubert Pierlot, fled to France establishing a government in exile in Bordeaux. Sadly, this was not to last long as France fell to the Nazis, and in May 1940 the exiled government sought refuge in London taking up residence in Eaton Square. The first and foremost concern was the 15,000 Belgians who had fled to Britain with few resources and were in need. A central service was set up to support them. Material support was offered and a service to help find the refugees employment. Four schools were set up: in Kingston, Buxton, Braemar and Penrith.

One well known Belgian refugee at this time was Ralph Miliband who fled with his father to this country.[2] On arrival he found work with a furniture removers, rescuing furniture from bombed houses. He was much moved by the sight of poverty in London's East End and it was this experience that confirmed his views as a socialist. He then managed to gain a place at the London School of Economics (LSE) under Harold Laski but in 1943 joined the Royal Navy to contribute to the war effort. He continued his academic career after the war, eventually becoming a professor. The family name has become known through his sons David and Ed. Ed became leader of the Labour Party in opposition from 2010–15.

David, previously a Foreign Secretary under Tony Blair, moved to work for the International Rescue Committee, a refugee-based organisation in New York in 2015.

Those Dutch refugees who could escape also came in mid-May 1940. There were approximately 23,000 German nationals living in Holland when the Nazis invaded and many were Jewish exiles. As they were ordered to be confined to their homes by the occupying forces, any chance of escape for them had to be last minute.

Any journey to Britain was to be across the perilous North Sea. On 17 May, a group of fourteen arrived at the coast, only to find the last refugee rescue ship had left. In desperation they cycled to Scheveningen, where they managed to take a sailing boat: a small vessel that none of them had sailed on before. After fourteen hours through churning seas in this tiny boat, they were rescued by a Dutch coastal vessel and taken to England. Jewish members were taken to a police station for investigation.

Another refugee who escaped by sea was a doctor who showed his stethoscope as proof of his profession. He described travelling in a lifeboat designed for twenty people but which carried thirty-seven in all. (From the Huguenots crossing from France in fishing smacks, to the Basque ship, *Habana*, overcrowded with children we see that the refugee crossing to England by sea has always been hazardous. It is a measure dictated by fear. Tragically we see similar crossings undertaken currently in the Mediterranean Sea and the English Channel.)

In London, these and other refugees were looked after by the Netherlands Emergency Committee which was composed of the Dutch church in London and the Dutch Benevolent Society. Initial accommodation was arranged at the Bonnington Hotel in Holborn (which proved quite expensive), and subsequently for twenty-seven refugees at Bernard Street. The Bonnington Hotel continued to act as a social centre for the refugees. The Netherlands Emergency Committee folded after two years but its work was continued by the Dutch Red Cross.

After Poland fell, the Polish airmen regrouped first in Romania before moving onto France. It was their intention to fight alongside French forces but when that country also fell to the Nazis, they managed to escape to the UK.

It was here that their expertise in the aerial bombing of German targets was much appreciated and as we shall see the government here rewarded them with support and citizenship after the war.

The real war became apparent as Hitler unleashed the Blitzkrieg on major British cities. For refugees who had arrived in the UK before war broke out, life was precarious: they were in a strange country and many had anxieties about people left behind. However, they had the advantage of support. At the outbreak of war, Jewish charities were running out of money so the government agreed to take this over. It seems that monies paid out were not simply at a flat rate. One Jewish lady refugee with physical and mental problems received a weekly addition of 1 shilling for a special diet. Interestingly such a payment was reintroduced under Supplementary Benefit but abolished in 1988 when the Conservative government changed the benefit system to one of Income Support.

With a substantial foreign population in the country the government resorted to a policy of internment in May 1940. For some time they had been unsure what to do with the increasing number of refugees from enemy alien countries. The fear was that there could be Nazi infiltrators among those refugees, hiding behind their status. Existing residents from enemy countries such as Germany and Italy were also included in the internment plan. There had been hesitation about introducing this policy but it was enacted in May 1940, once Churchill replaced Chamberlain as prime minister.

For the 70,000 Jewish refugees who had made it to the UK at the beginning of the war, life was not easy and was about to become rather more difficult.

Tribunals were set up across the country to assess whether people should be interned.[3] They had the power to intern or exempt from internment. Their biggest interests were in people of German and Austrian origin and they were looking for people who would be susceptible to pressure from enemy agents. Effectively they were testing people's moral character and making judgements to see if they could be pressurised. Each tribunal would consist of a chairman, a policeman and preferably a woman.

They could make one of three decisions:

Class A – suspected of Nazi sympathies and interned immediately.

Class B – restricted freedom when considered immediate internment unnecessary.

Class C – recognised as genuine refugee from Nazi oppression.

The numbers interned were high. The Central Committee for Refugees stated that in June 1942 there were 3,222; in May, 4,197 people were interned.

People, including children as young as 16, were sent to various internment centres, the largest being on the Isle of Man. For children there were also centres at Belfast, Nottingham, Oxford and Walsall. One at Shefford in Bedfordshire was found to be unsanitary and was closed down. Lack of facilities meant that in Skelmorlie in Scotland the young refugees were mixed with evacuees.

Anyone over 16 could be sent to British colonies to ease overcrowding. These could be as far away as Canada or Australia. Many considered this policy too harsh and were horrified when the *Arandora Star* was torpedoed on its way to Canada with the loss of hundreds of refugee lives. Even then, further internees, including the survivors from the *Arandora Star,* were shipped to Australia.

The following is a case example and concerns Ken Ambrose, originally called Kurt.

As a young Jewish boy in Stettin (Szczecin), Poland, near the Baltic Sea, Ken had been sent by his parents to the King's School in Taunton, Somerset where a Jewish teacher, Ludwig Rosenberg from Berlin, had been invited to teach by the headmaster in 1934. In 1940, Ken found himself swept up by internment and placed at a camp at Lingfield racecourse. Subsequently he was one of those transported to Australia on HMT *Dunera* (an old Boer war ship) and interned at the Hay camp there. Eventually, on returning to the UK, he took part in the war effort as an officer with the RAF, working on the bombing survey in Great Britain and north-west Europe.

Lucy Masterman papers lodged in the Cadbury Collection, Birmingham University[3]

In Cambridge, Lucy Masterman worked tirelessly on behalf of refugees both before and during the war. She was a humanitarian and had been an active member of the Women's Federation of Housing Associations in Battersea, south-west London. She had contested the Salisbury parliamentary seat in the General Election and come second. When internment began, she was influential in advocating on behalf of interned refugees whilst continuing her work for those in community.

The papers contain some interesting case studies. It should be stated that children as young as 16 could be dealt with under the internment rules. Most children were placed in hostels but some were given individual help. For instance, one boy, Ludwig Herbst, was boarded out in Penzance so he could visit a dying relative. Ludwig was given full financial support. He was accompanied by an adult helper who was awarded 75 per cent of his own costs. A very promising girl student was supported so that she could attend Exeter University.

A Jewish lady photographer with an Aryan employer had had to leave Germany because the servant had threatened to betray her but now living in England she had been interned.

At Lord Waldegrave's manor near Bath, one lady was pleading for her husband to obtain forestry work so he could be released from internment. But the answer was that since the lord had to lay off staff because of war taxation he therefore could not take on anyone else. The wife's letter is literally pleading and is a tragic reflection of the effect of this internment policy. It shows too that marriage to an English woman didn't save him from internment.

Many people, particularly those who mixed in influential circles, were strongly opposed to the policy of internment and particularly the dangerous practice of sending refugees on boats to the colonies. The economist John Maynard Keynes was vocal in his campaign against the policy and advocated for several economist colleagues. Francois Lafitte, an activist who had been in the Communist Party at Oxford and who worked for the PEP was asked to write a pamphlet protesting the policy by Leonard Elmhirst of Dartington College and chairman of the PEP. A number of Dartington staff had been interned. Lafitte's impassioned tract *The Internment of Aliens* was directed at the government in the form of Herbert Morrison the new Home Secretary.

It was not only refugees from Germany who suffered the fate of internment. Eduardo Paolozzi was an Italian, born in Scotland in 1924.

When war broke out, aged 16, he was interned for three months as an enemy alien with his father and uncle.

Tragically his father and uncle were deported on the *Arandora Star* with all lives lost. In the year 2000, as a well-known sculptor, his Faraday sculpture was installed on the campus at Birmingham University not far from the Cadbury collection, which records the stories of refugee internments and their advocate Lucy Masterman from Cambridge.

As well as Eduardo, many other foreign nationals already resident here came to be interned, and such was the fate of many resident refugees. In August 1940, an Aliens Order closed the county of Devon to all Germans and in the same month adopted a wholesale policy of internment for all German and Austrian refugees.

At Dartington College in Devon, which inspired LaFitte's pamphlet, they advocated for individual refugees who worked there.[4] One of these was Ann Fernbach, a young woman with a baby who was a skilled potter and who had worked with Bernard Leach. Others, including Hans Oppenheimer, who had been director of music at Dartington, were sent to the Dixons Internment Camp in nearby Paignton. Hans was visited but visitors were not allowed to see him personally. Their only contact was with an adjutant who gave no individual information about him. There was great concern for his health since he was diabetic and the general internment diet was starch. It looks like their advocacy was successful since he was released on ill-health grounds in July 1940.

Wilhelm Soukop had been interned in Canada. Correspondence from a companion says they had been terrified of being torpedoed on the way over and 'now they are staying under canvas and behind barbed wire'.

The semblance of a full-blown prison camp is palpable. The next entry is better news: Soukop is returning to the UK and has a reference to teach. It is noted that he is an accomplished artist and has previously exhibited in London.

Leonard Elmhirst and his wife Dorothy's reputation of helping interned refugees and others became known and they were approached for help with children crossing into the country. These children were coming from a number of countries which included Germany itself, Austria, Poland, Czechoslovakia and the Free Port of Danzig. Some were able to come by regular train routes but the children of anti-Nazi fighters had to be smuggled across the Czech/Polish border, leaving parents behind in prisons. Crossing the border meant travelling in deep snow at night and the little ones had to be doped so they didn't cry out and alert the Gestapo guards. Once they reached the UK, they were found foster parents but even that stability could be jeopardised if they were in a protected area, e.g. Devon, as they would have to move again.

A committee had been formed including the German League of Culture in Great Britain, the Council of Austrians in Great Britain, the Refugee Teachers' Association and youth organisations representing Austria, Germany and Czechoslovakia.

All of these wanted Leonard Elmhirst to join the committee but although he was keen, he said the distance from Devon would make it difficult to fully participate. They wanted many of the children to re-emigrate to the US but Leonard made them aware that the Americans would stipulate they would only take the children if they could be returned after the war. The willingness to help children, as with adult refugees, was tempered by the need to move them on.

Whilst the government gradually ran down the policy of internment, we can see from the Central Committee for refugees contained in the Lucy Masterman papers that many were still interned in mid-1942. The government could not simply free them but needed to go through a form of judicial release. The internees needed to show that not only that they were no threat to security but that their release would in some way assist the war effort. This was much more difficult to demonstrate. As enemy aliens the ex-internees could not be conscripted but could be offered a route out through joining the Army's Auxiliary Military Pioneers Corp. The new Home Secretary Herbert Morrison favoured this.

Another route out of internment was via re-immigration. Many people had come to Britain as a route to moving on later and some had papers to support this. The instruction had been that such people should not have been interned but many had been swept up in the process. As people left their internment camps, those with papers for the US were accompanied to the port to ensure they left. In time, this somewhat draconian method was tempered in the regulations. However, it is believed that many of the 10,000 refugees who left at this time were not volunteers in the strictest sense. Herbert Emmerson, High Commissioner for Refugees, agreed that if people with papers were able to emigrate they should do so. There would be no further financial assistance if they did not leave.

Government Policy towards the Jews

Once the war started, the admission of endangered Jews from the continent was not considered government responsibility. Any refugees arriving from enemy alien countries would be strictly vetted as a potential risk. As early as 25 September 1939, the government considered that the only way of solving the problem was in pursuing the war and defeating Nazi Germany. This was logical as an aim but no help for those trying to escape the terror in Germany and all its occupied territories.

Schemes to assist the exit from Nazi-occupied countries were contemplated by the international community, including European countries, but all were considered to have unwarranted and unpredictable risks.

Notwithstanding this assessment, the plight of Jews left in the occupied territories was of great concern. Francis Meynell, then working at the Board of Trade, commissioned a Gallup poll asking people's views on allowing Jewish people entrance to the UK.[5] Seventy-eight per cent favoured admission, of which 40 per cent wanted admission just until people could be found safe refuge elsewhere, 28 per cent favoured refuge until the end of the war and 10 per cent approved permanent refuge in Britain.

Inspired by Victor Gollanz's book *Let My People Go*, Meynell organised a group of sympathetic people to campaign for an open-door policy to help save people. Included in the group were Gollanz, Rathbone, Dennis Cohen, Alan Sainsbury, Mrs Reginald McKenna, Sydney Bernstein and Tom Driberg MP. They wanted to set up camps to receive people who could escape and to challenge anti-Semitic views in this country. The results of Meynell's poll were widely publicised and the government and newspapers received many letters in support of allowing admission of Jews fleeing the Nazis. The government acknowledged it had received many letters but its position was hardly changed. By March 1943, a debate in the Lords saw an impassioned plea from the Archbishop of Canterbury for a policy of rescue but Lord Cranborne rebuked him for only being interested in Jewish refugees and the matter was taken no further.[6]

Later, when Emerson, the High Commissioner for Refugees, learnt of plans for 'the final solution' he began to push for further steps, but the progress of individual cases did not proceed well, due to the length of the process. It has often been said that the terrible story of the concentration camps, and before them mobile extermination units, was not known until the Allied troops liberated Germany and Poland in 1945.[7] Sadly, this is not true: as far back as June 1942 there were graphic and credible accounts of what was happening in the occupied territories. These were printed in the *Daily Telegraph* on 25 June and came from Szmul Zygielbojm, a Jew and member of the Polish government in exile. He wanted the world to know what was happening to Jews under Nazi occupation and those supplying him the information undertook great risks. The story in the *Daily Telegraph* was smuggled to London on microfiche hidden in a key. The newspaper was able to report that gas chambers were being used for industrialised murder from November 1941 onwards and that 1,000 Jews were being gassed every day. It lists the death toll from massacres in seven different towns and cities. Often Jews were deported from the cities to unknown destinations and then taken into the nearby woods and shot en-masse. In Vilna, 50,000 Jews were murdered and in Lithuanian Kovno, the total number was 300,000.

David Blair (*Daily Telegraph*, 26 January 2015) reported that during the war, the *Daily Telegraph* chose to report this terrible account only on page five of the newspaper. Nevertheless, the information was available to the government and must have informed many of those members of the public who wrote pleading with the government to do something.

Zygielbojm was passionate about making the government and people aware of what was going on in the Nazi-occupied territories, expecting action to stop the slaughter. He sent telegrams to both Churchill and Roosevelt but to no avail. His wife and son were still stuck in the Warsaw ghetto and when that was razed to the ground, they perished alongside everyone else.

Crushed by this personal tragedy and the indifference towards the fate of the Jews he took his own life in London on 11 May 1943. He wrote:

The responsibility for the crime of the murder of the whole Jewish
nationality rests first on those who are carrying it out. But indirectly
it falls upon the whole of humanity, on the peoples of the Allied
nations and on their governments who up to this day have not taken
any real steps to halt this crime. By looking on passively upon this
murder of defenceless millions of tortured children, women and
men they are becoming partners to this responsibility.

Under pressure from the Archbishop of Canterbury and members of the
public a conference to look at the issue of Jews in occupied territory was
called jointly by the British and Americans in April 1943.[8] Held in the
balmy climes of Bermuda it couldn't have been further from the Nazi
carnage across Europe. From the beginning, the choice of delegates
indicated the lack of priority considered: Britain was represented
by Richard Law, a junior minister at the Foreign Office of no great
importance in Churchill's government and the Americans sent Harold
Dodd, president of Princeton University. The premise was to approach
Hitler through an intermediary to see if he would let numbers of Jews
leave Germany. One objection made was if Hitler were to let people go
he would be likely to hide Nazis amongst the group sent. It was also
believed that he simply wouldn't let people go, therefore any attempt at
negotiation was a waste of time. It is said though that the conference was
worried that Hitler just might agree and that Britain and America would
not be able to cope with the results. The only resolutions discussed were
to try and get Jewish people who had already escaped Nazi Germany
into neutral territory in North Africa but there was no coherent plan.
An American delegate, who was himself Jewish, promoted more positive
measures but he was voted down.

  Zygielbojm was aware of the lack of action from this conference when
he took his own life in London in May 1943. He was devastated by their
indifference.

  As Zygielbojm knew in 1943, the murderous nature of the Nazi regime
would roll on and by then could not be stemmed by British and indeed
American passivity. In some ways the die had been cast in the 1930s when
Britain, wanting good trade relations with Germany, failed to offer robust
criticism of that country. During the course of the Spanish Civil War,

adopting a non-intervention policy gave Hitler the green light to support Franco in such actions as the bombing of Guernica. We have seen that the government continued to believe, or perhaps it is fair to say, wanted to believe, that Hitler would not invade any more countries.

The results were tragic in the extreme, millions killed on the battlefield and 6 million Jews, with others not considered worthy, tortured and killed in the concentration camps.

The following story of Rudolph Becker (known to his family and friends as Rudi) was provided by Sara Elizabeth Smiles, a friend and fellow student of the author.

Born in Berlin, Germany in 1910, Rudi was the only child of Max and his wife Erna. They ran a very successful high-class tailoring and dress-making business and counted Marlene Dietrich amongst their patrons. After the Great War, Berlin, under the Weimar Republic, flourished in the fields of science, architecture, music, film, higher education, government and military affairs. Film and drama were important features of the cultural life of the state. The fact that Marlene Dietrich had her clothes made by the Beckers demonstrated how close they were to an inner circle of the Berlin elite. Other actresses would have followed the iconic fashion styles of her film *The Blue Angel*.

The growing Fascist movement within Berlin and the wider country disapproved of the life in Berlin considering it to be 'decadent'. Joseph Goebbels became City Gauleiter (the Nazi Party's district leader) in 1926 and in his first week in office deliberately provoked violence in a working-class area by organising a march through that district. Local people sought to confront the fascists and the ensuing street battle foreshadowed later events.

Following the worldwide economic crash of 1928, life for everyone became increasingly difficult. The Nazis used people's discontent to scapegoat different groups and from 1933 onwards, Jewish people became subject to a barrage of oppressive laws. These included laws made by the Nazi regime which systematically stripped Jewish people of their positions in the civil and government service. A test of Jewish ancestry was applied, which meant anyone with Jewish blood would also be deprived of their academic tenure in universities. It was inherent in Nazi ideology that the economic misery suffered by the German people was directly the result of the Jewish ownership and control of businesses and therefore they sought to appropriate Jewish businesses.

The Nazis declared Jewish people to be second-class citizens and under the Nuremberg Laws of April 1933 they removed German nationality from Jewish people. This is what happened to Rudi and his family.

Rudi was the only son and became involved in the family tailoring business. The family owned a shop in Berlin and also one in Monaco, the latter run by Rudi. This was in the early 1930s.

The exact details of what happened to the family businesses is not known; suffice to say that eventually they were all sequestrated by the Nazi regime. It appears that the family later ended up designing and making the suits worn by the SA (Stormtroopers). This was obviously due to the quality of their workmanship and it seems likely that they had no choice. Records of the family business have not been located so far.

The information handed down to Sara is that sometime around 1938, with the Nazi grip tightening and the oppression of Jewish people escalating, Rudi and his parents crossed the border to the west thereby escaping Nazi Germany and perhaps working out a route for the rest of the family to follow. Rudi proceeded to England and lived homeless for a while on the South Bank in London. Erna died not long after arriving in England. It appears that his father, Max, later returned to the family in Berlin; there is no record as to why he made this journey but it is surmised that he intended to help his extended family escape. In the event Max and all ninety-six members of the extended family were never seen again.

It is known that Rudi was living in Britain by 1941, since in that year he met and married Vera in Islington, London. Within the family this was considered a great love match as the couple had met on an underground platform in London during the Blitz. Rudi had by now changed his name, anglicising it from Rudolph Becker to Robert Baker-Byrne. He took his wife's family name which is Irish in origin.

Records show that Rudi later found employment with the Pioneer Corps (Army Auxiliary Military Pioneer Corps or AMPC). Interestingly many young Jewish men, barred from joining the regular British forces, were encouraged to join this corps.

From the Pioneer Corps he was recruited into a secret unit called 'Twelve Force' (staffed primarily by Jewish refugees), whose role was to travel clandestinely behind enemy lines into Germany by plane in order to sabotage key German military installations. After the war ended and the concentration camps were liberated, Rudi was employed in a significant role in collecting evidence against the Nazis, for example, by collecting shoes taken from prisoners in the death camps. He was accompanied by his wife and small daughter, who lived in Berlin. Aged 49 he played another significant role by providing evidence at the Nuremberg trials. He died in 1964 aged 54. The doctor told his widow that given Rudi's life experiences and the strain they had put on his heart that he was surprised that Rudi had lasted so long.

The story has been handed down through the family and Sara and other siblings wish to carry out further archival research about their remarkable grandfather.

Chapter 11

The Displacement of Peoples
after the Second World War

The Second World War resulted in one of the biggest displacements of people in human history. There were people who had fled the Nazis as they advanced across Europe and other parts of the world and many others who had been forced eastwards by the Soviet forces. In February 1945 and with the defeat of Nazi Germany considered inevitable, the three great powers, America, Russia and Britain (represented by Franklin D. Roosevelt, Joseph Stalin and Winston Churchill) met at Yalta, in the Ukraine, to discuss how post-war Europe would be organised – most notably the partition of Germany. The agreements – not all of which were honoured – shaped European politics for the next five decades. It was deemed that the best solution to the mass migration of people was to ensure that people could return to their own regions as quickly as possible. However, when the war finally ended in May 1945, it rapidly became clear that there were often insurmountable obstacles to achieving this. Many borders and national boundaries had been redrawn and people's former homes had been occupied by others or destroyed.

Over a million refugees could not be repatriated to their original countries and were left homeless as a result of the fear of persecution. These included:

Ethnic or religious groups that were likely to be persecuted in their countries of origin. These included a large number of Jewish people, many of whom were survivors from the concentration camps, and others.

Poles, Ukrainians and some Czechs, who feared persecution by the communist regimes installed in their home countries by the Soviet army: in particular those from provinces that had been recently incorporated into the Soviet Union.

Estonians and Latvians whose homelands had been invaded by the Soviet Union (1940) and remained occupied after the war. Croats, Serbs and Slovenes who feared persecution by the communist government established by Tito.

Citizens of the Free City of Danzig annexed by Poland (1945).

The Soviet Union insisted that all peoples who were originally 'their' citizens be repatriated. American, British, and French military officials, as well as United Nations Relief and Rehabilitation Administration (UNRRA) officials, reluctantly complied with this directive, and a number of Soviet citizens were repatriated. Many of these met with the hardship they feared, including death and confinement in the gulags. There were also cases of kidnapping and coercion to return these refugees. Many avoided such repatriation by misrepresenting their origins, fleeing, or simply resisting. The Western powers rejected the Soviet's claim for sovereignty over the Baltic States and allied officials also refused to repatriate Lithuanian, Estonian, and Latvian refugees against their will. Similarly, a large number of refugees who were repatriated to Yugoslavia were subjected to summary executions and torture.

Many Poles, who later agreed to be repatriated, did in fact suffer arrest and some were executed, particularly those that had served in the Warsaw Uprising of 1944, or in the Polish Resistance against the Nazis.

Jewish survivors of the death camps and various work camps refused to return to their countries of origin, starting instead an extensive underground movement to migrate to Palestine.

Jewish Holocaust survivors typically could not return to their former homes because these no longer existed or had been appropriated by former neighbours; the few Eastern European Jews who returned often experienced renewed anti-Semitism.

In 1945, most Jewish Holocaust survivors had little choice but to stay in the displaced persons' camps; most Jewish people who wanted to could not leave Europe because Britain had severely limited legitimate Jewish immigration to Palestine and illegal immigration was strongly curtailed. Jewish refugees hoping to reach other countries, including the US, also met with restrictions and quotas.

Resettlement of Displaced Persons

Preparations for mass resettlement had been undertaken during the war. There had been fears that the movement of people could block Allied advances and also transmit diseases such as typhus.[1] In May 1944, a displaced persons branch of military government was established to control their movement. Arrangements were made in November 1944, with the Relief and Rehabilitation Fund, for teams to work with the military for the care of displaced persons. The use of military barracks, some of which were former work or concentration camps, shaped the post-war refugee resettlement. Relief workers from various British agencies had been working with Allied armies for the care of displaced people throughout the war. There were 1,500 voluntary relief workers in the British zone of Germany by July 1945. These included the Red Cross, Jewish Committee for Relief Abroad, Scouts and Guides International, Catholic Committee for Relief Abroad, Salvation Army, Save the Children Fund, Quaker Friends and more. There was much debate about how best to assist and support these displaced people. It was recognised that this would not just be material support; so many people had suffered so much and therefore also needed social, psychological and spiritual support. Concern was expressed that camps separated by nationality would foster isolation and a competitive ethos. Some teams concentrated on running social and work-related schemes not just to alleviate boredom but to prevent dependency. Workers called for fewer camps and people being rehoused in communities but they recognised the challenge of the terrible housing conditions: a consequence of wartime bombing. In the British section in Germany, for example, only two-thirds of former dwellings were considered habitable. Other refugees and displaced workers were brought to Britain after the war, under the European Volunteer Worker Scheme. Britain was short of workers, and officials from the Ministry of Labour were sent to the displaced persons camps to recruit people to work in key occupations in industry and farming and the newly formed National Health Service.

It is worth mentioning that when British officials visited the displaced persons camps across Europe that conditions were often unsatisfactory. Some had no proper beds, the food was minimal and the huts suffered infestations. At one place, it was so bad that inhabitants had started to steal and slaughter cattle. They had also stolen a horse and were using it to sell for food on the black-market. Seeing those conditions, people would have been grateful to escape to the UK. However, their perception differed from that of the British who saw them primarily as workers. They considered themselves refugees from a subjugated state which had first been overrun by the Nazis and then by the Soviet Union.[2] They were expected to learn English but many were not so keen to make the effort as they expected to return home in good time. Sadly, it was not until the late 1980s that the former Soviet Union collapsed allowing free movement to the Baltic States.

Once it became obvious that repatriation plans omitted a large number of displaced persons who needed new homes, it took time for countries to commit to the acceptance of refugees. Existing refugee quotas were completely inadequate, and by the autumn of 1946, it was not clear whether the remaining displaced persons would ever find a home.

However, between 1947 and 1953, the vast majority of the 'non-repatriables' would find new homes around the world. A number of countries accepted displaced people, usually to assist with internal labour schemes. These included Belgium, Canada, Australia, Venezuela, Brazil, Argentina, French Morocco, Iraq and Norway. The US did eventually accept displaced people but it was not until three years after the war had ended and so much later than many other countries. In order to have some of these refugees come to the US, President Truman asked Congress to enact legislation.

Truman's administration, along with a lobbying group for refugees, Citizens Committee on Displaced Persons, favoured allowing European refugees from the Second World War to enter the US. Truman signed the first Displaced Persons Act on 25 June 1948. It allowed 200,000 displaced people to enter the country within the following two years. However, in the end they exceeded the quota by extending the Act for another two years, which doubled the admission of refugees into the US to 415,000. So it was that from 1949 to 1952, about half the 900,000 immigrants that entered the US were those displaced by the war. In order to qualify for American visas, only those who had been in internment camps by the end of 1945 were eligible. The displaced people trying to come to America had to have a sponsor and a place to live before their arrival. The UK accepted 86,000 displaced people as part of various 'labour import' programmes, the largest being 'Operation Westward Ho'. This scheme was designed to bring people to work in agriculture, forestry, coal mining and cotton textiles.

These came in addition to 115,000 Polish army veterans, who had joined the Polish Resettlement Corps, plus 12,000 former members of the Waffen SS from the Ukrainian 'Halychyna Division'. Heinrich Himmler had allowed these Ukrainians from Galicia to join the crack Nazi regiment because he considered them to have features akin to the Aryan race. It is claimed that the Foreign Office, at the time, had found it a hopeless task to screen the 8,000 men, who surrendered to the British and were held at Rimini after the war.

However, they had refused to return them to Soviet Russia and instead allowed them to settle in Britain – despite Home Office misgivings about potential war criminals amongst their ranks. Many continued to live in the UK while others moved on to Canada and Australia. (It is unclear to the author the full reasoning for their acceptance into Britain.)

Another project aimed at young single women from the Baltic States was dubbed the 'Balt Cygnets'.[3] A quaint, somewhat sexist phrase which would not be used nowadays, expected the women to be scrupulously clean in their habits and full of the 'spirit and stuff' of which 'we can make Britons'. They were assigned to domestic service or hospital work.

The conditions of service for women to be included in the Balt Cygnets programme between 1946 and 1947 are available for scrutiny. They required the women to be employed at British hospitals or similar institutions and to be 18 to 40 years of age, or up to 50 if they could prove their physical fitness.

Initially they would be involved in basic domestic work but those with previous nursing experience could apply for a position after three months and if accepted could train for a nursing or midwifery post. They could be placed in any type of institution, the exception being the sanatoria. If they breached their conditions they could be returned to the camp from whence they came. Their pay would be the same as British workers at that grade but they could not change employment within their initial first year visa. They would be required to carry identification at all times and also received food and clothing vouchers. In retrospect it appears that these conditions were in some measure a form of social engineering.

Latvian women in particular were considered of 'sound stock and admirable partners' for British men, as their reproduction would ensure a healthy white British line. The arrival of the *Empire Windrush* in 1948, carrying migrants from Jamaica, happened almost in parallel and the story of Polish refugees arriving on the same boat is told below.

Many of the refugees could only travel to Britain after the Nazis were defeated. One of the most interesting but gruelling journeys was made by the Poles. In a pact with the Nazis in 1939, Stalin divided their country and forced 1.5 million people from their homes and into Siberian work camps. Many perished from the terrible conditions of overwork, hunger and severe cold. One group escaped and around 1,000 people managed to survive the 3,000-mile journey into Iran where they were welcomed. A most remarkable feat.

From there many had safe passage into India which at that time was still ruled by the British Empire. From Iran and other countries, groups of refugees were gathered up to be returned to Europe. One intriguing aspect is the sixty-six Polish people who travelled to London with people from Jamaica on HMT *Empire Windrush*.

In 1998, the author visited an exhibition about the *Windrush* at the Museum of London, fifty years after its arrival. She was fascinated at the time to see a small but significant group of passengers who had originated in Mexico but clearly were of Eastern European origin. The exhibition showed details of addresses these Polish people had intended to move to in the UK but that information was not retained. It is only now that journalists have written about this story.

An American academic, Nicholas Boston, followed up the story of one Polish group from the *Windrush*.[4] In the summer of 1943, 1,400 Poles, mainly women and children, who had been displaced by the Russian aggression during the war, were transported to Colonia Santa Rosa, a refugee village in Mexico. There they stayed until 1947 when the Polish Resettlement Act was passed in Britain. Some would be transported by other countries but this group of sixty-six Polish people were picked up by the *Windrush* on its way to Jamaica.

To illustrate this scenario, here is the case of Stefania Nowak who was 28 years of age on 21 June 1948 when she disembarked the HMT *Empire Windrush* at Tilbury Harbour. Journalists were on site to interview the ship's passengers, not Nowak, but 494 West Indians who had made the journey to seek jobs in the post-war economy.

Those first news reports were early wordings of the *Windrush* narrative, which posits that these arrivals, in taking a step that greater numbers from the colonial West Indies and postcolonial Caribbean would follow, are progenitors of today's African-Caribbean community. Nowak belonged to a different migration that was then underway. Hers was the result of a government-sponsored scheme to gather Polish nationals scattered across the globe and reunite them with partners and families in the UK. This slice of British-Polish history is well documented and celebrated. However, the unique significance of Nowak's specific journey – its intersection with another community's historical trajectory – has received little attention.

In all there were thirty-nine adult women, twenty-six children and a Polish man. The people had already been allocated camps to go to: Shobdon near Leominster; Camp Blackshaw in Staffordshire; Lynn Park Aberdeen and Roughan Camp near Bury St Edmunds. Employment was allocated to each person and in the case of the women they were allocated work via a codename 'HD' which largely meant domestic work.

For almost as many of the ones who became British, there were others – at least twenty-seven, according to available records – who moved on to Canada or the US. Amongst this batch was Stefania Nowak. The Nowaks departed Britain on 24 November 1948 for Canada aboard the *Empress of France*. Their entries on that ship's passenger list give their 'last address in the UK' as simply 'c/o War Office, London'. For Stefania's occupation: 'Housewife'. She died in Hamilton, Ontario, on 17 December 2012, aged 92.

The British government had allowed these Polish people to travel to Britain on the *Windrush* so as to reunite wives with their husbands. Many stayed in Britain, put down roots and spent their working life here. Others using Britain as a staging post re-emigrated to the US or Canada. Many

Poles in Europe including ex-service men could not return home to a country where the regime was so markedly changed, now under control of the Soviet bloc. The British government agreed to take responsibility for Polish service men and refugees. They remembered the invaluable help that regrouped service personnel had afforded Britain during the war.

In 1946, the Polish Resettlement Corps was founded.[5] Polish ex-servicemen could be helped via the corps to retrain and receive education that would help them settle into UK life. An agreement was made with British trade unions that Polish workers could only be recruited through the corps and placed into approved Ministry of Labour jobs. In 1947, the Polish Resettlement Act enshrined these arrangements in law and proved a landmark piece of legislation. It aimed to resettle and integrate political refugees and outlined the help and support which would be given to Polish refugees. This included an entitlement to employment and to unemployment benefits. It also laid out the responsibilities of government departments to provide health services, pension entitlements and education.

The Act, in itself, was considered a work of great statesmanship and because it contained such supportive measures to facilitate integration it helped people's acceptance of the newcomers. It also provided a much-needed additional labour force to help Britain's post-war recovery. By the end of 1949, around 150,000 Polish people had settled in Britain and were working hard. They formed the basis of the thriving Polish population in Britain today.

It was the first time that legislation of this kind had been introduced solely in support of a particular refugee group and it demonstrated that by providing adequate resources and responding positively to the needs of a refugee group the integration process into the host society could be significantly eased and effective. Much work was taken up accommodating Polish refugees. Polish Resettlement Camps utilised former army and air force bases, and by October 1946, around 120,000 Polish troops had been quartered in 265 camps across the country.

In the following years, wives and dependants were brought to join them giving a total population of 249,000. The huts were in remote places and had bare facilities. There were electric lights and slow combustion stoves.

Education was a priority and in 1947 the Committee for the Education of Poles was set up. Its principal aim was to 'fit the Poles for absorption into British schools and careers whilst still maintaining provision for their natural desire for the maintenance of Polish culture and knowledge of Polish history and literature'. It was to be funded out of monies supplied by parliament.

The Home Secretary announced that Polish ex-servicemen could apply for British citizenship from March 1948. Through their contribution to the war effort and their hard work in Britain this group of refugees had been assimilated.

The Children

Perhaps the most tragic aspect of those people who survived the war were the children of the Holocaust.[6] In the concentration camps most had lost parents, siblings and often extended family as well. They had suffered severe privation, often torture and witnessed unspeakable cruelties to others.

In addition, they had no home to return to. Doing something to support at least a group of these children became imperative. At the end of the war a British philanthropist called Leonard Montefiore, on behalf of the Committee for the Care of Children from the Concentration Camps, persuaded the government to accept 1,000 such children. In the event it was 732 children, of whom just 80 were girls, who made their way to the UK. Of those, it was decided that 300 children would sent to Windermere in the Lake District to benefit from its seclusion and peaceful nature. The stories of some of those survivors bears testimony to their ability to survive unimaginable horrors but also to the opportunities and support they found in post-war Britain. These things didn't come easily. The boys enjoyed sports, playing, swimming in the lake and, for the first time, decent food. Their physical health blossomed but the memories troubled them particularly at night when they lay still in the bunk beds, and screams often echoed throughout the dormitory. The memories were too terrible to share even with their peers. Even as their bodies filled out there was still something physical they could not erase: their concentration camp number embedded on their arm. After their stay, they were dispersed to cities around the country to learn trades. By 2015, only fifty of the original boys were thought to be alive but they remain in contact and endeavour to hold a reunion each year, along with the other remaining child refugees who came from Prague in 1945. Traumatic tales gradually emerged and were documented by a reporter from the *Daily Telegraph*. One Polish man explained how, as a young boy, his mother and 8-year-old sister were executed in 1943, after which he and his father were transferred to Buchenwald concentration camp in Germany. The next move for him was to a nearby camp where he was starved and brutalised whilst making anti-tank weapons. Then his father was shot trying to escape a death march. He felt this so strongly, thinking his father had been killed like a dog in the middle of nowhere, and it continued to prey on his mind.

Another man recounted how as a boy he had lost eighty-one members of his close and extended family, including his mother who was gassed and buried in a mass grave. At the age of 15 in July 1944 he was sent to Auschwitz. He was in a barracks with 100 bunks which were shared by 1,000 men. Rations were extremely meagre, a piece of black bread and black coffee made from burnt wheat, with a watery soup for lunch and nothing else. If the guards noticed any sign of weakness, inmates would be despatched to the gas chambers. Just four days before liberation, they were taken out and put on a forced march to Buchenwald. It was January but they were only wearing pyjamas with no hats or wooden clogs. Anyone who was seen to be failing was shot in the back of the head and left lying there.

Those days in Windermere were a balm to their previous existences. They swam, they played volleyball and football and they ran a little wild, borrowing bikes that were not locked and careering round the countryside. They sneaked into the cinema in Windermere to watch Errol Flynn and Jeanette MacDonald. Their bodies filled out as they ate proper meals. But the lack of food they had endured meant they often secreted bread rolls under their mattresses.

Now in their eighties many still obsess about food. Most have had successful lives in Britain.

One went on to represent this country in weightlifting twice at the Olympic Games. The first time, in 1956, was just eleven years after he had emerged from the camps as an emaciated boy.

Another had had such traumatic experiences that he could not speak about it for fifty years. However, when he came to write a book this act helped him to do so. Sadly, that inability to speak even to those closest is not uncommon. It adds a further burden to their suffering.

Chapter 9 described how when the Nazis came to power they unleashed their vitriolic hate on the Jews and others designated as inferior and disposable. At the end of the war, Hitler's dream of establishing a 1,000-year Reich was in tatters but the hurt caused was unimaginable. These boys and other displaced people were victims whose lives he and his fascist regime had shattered. Their memory lives on in the Lakes where a permanent exhibition arranged by the Lake District Holocaust Project is on show entitled: *We came from hell to paradise.*

Chapter 12

The Hungarian Uprising

T he aftermath of Second World War saw Eastern European countries fall under the political and military control of Soviet Union. These included East Germany, Czechoslovakia, Hungary, Yugoslavia, Romania, Poland, Bulgaria and Albania. Many displaced people from those countries had no desire to return to their homelands whilst the Soviets were in control. Equally, large numbers of the existing residents also were unhappy with Soviet governance and longed to escape.

In Hungary, economic wealth was leached from the country, leaving a poor standard of living for most Hungarians. A heavy-handed Soviet-backed police force kept people under control. But when Stalin died in 1953 and Khrushchev became leader, he began to make more liberal speeches, and Hungarian people hoped that repression would be lessened.

But in the autumn of 1956 when the students took to the streets, the troops were sent to quell them.[1] On the afternoon of 23 October, around 20,400 protesters gathered next to the statue of Jozef Bem, a Hungarian hero. The leader of the Writers' Union, Peter Veres, read a manifesto demanding an end to outside interference and the introduction of democratic socialism. A banned patriotic song extolling freedom was then sung and when someone in the crowd cut the Communist symbol, the hammer and sickle, out of the centre of the national flag many followed suite. The crowd crossed the Danube to join others at Parliament Square swelling the numbers to 200,000. Then at 8.00pm in the evening the First Secretary read a proclamation condemning the speeches and actions of the crowd.

Provoked by his hard-line rejection of any demands, a section of the multitude working together toppled the large statue of Stalin. A determined crowd marched on the offices of Radio Budapest calling for their demands to be broadcast. This was heavily guarded by the State

Protection Authority, Államvédelmi *Hatóság* (AVH), the Hungarian secret police. From inside the building, the AVH opened fire and a student was killed. His body was wrapped in the country's flag and held aloft. Outside the parliament, people were enraged and to quell the crowd the government sent in regular soldiers. This was not their best tactic since many soldiers tore their stars from their uniforms and sided with the protestors. The crowd fought back, incensed by the actions of the AVH: they set fire to cars, they seized guns from military establishments and released political prisoners.

The actions of the protesters led to the collapse of the government and the return to power of Imre Nagy, a leading communist official but a more open-minded Hungarian, as prime minister. The new government he led formally disbanded the AVH, declared its intention to withdraw from the Warsaw Pact and pledged to re-establish free elections. By the end of October, fighting had almost stopped, and a sense of normality began to return.

During the night, Secretary Erno Gero asked for intervention by their Soviet masters. Initially appearing open to negotiating a withdrawal of Soviet forces, the Soviet Politburo in Russia changed its mind and moved to crush the revolution. On 4 November, a large Soviet force invaded Budapest and other regions of the country. Hundreds of tanks were despatched to Budapest. In the ensuing repression 2,500 insurgents were killed. Echoing the strong fight back by local insurgents, Soviet troops suffered a loss of 700 men.

In the aftermath, thousands of Hungarians were arrested, with 28,000 being taken before the courts. Of those, 22,000 were sentenced and imprisoned; 1,300 were interned and 229 executed: 200,000 Hungarian nationals fled as refugees.

The Red Cross and Austrian army established refugee camps in Austria at Taiskirchen and Graz adjacent to the Hungarian border for those who wished to escape.

The Prime Minister, Imre Nagy, and others took refuge in the Yugoslavian Embassy but he was arrested as he tried to flee and was taken to Romania. In 1958, he was returned to Budapest and was executed after a secret show trial in June.

The events of October and November 1956 sent Hungarians fleeing from the repression. For those refugees who arrived in the UK at the end of that year there was a very warm welcome. The events in Budapest happened at the height of the Cold War with sympathies firmly on the side of those Hungarians who had challenged the Soviet Union. They were effectively the first refugees of a televisual age. For British people who owned a television set sympathy was evoked for these people who had escaped Russian tanks and were seen trudging through the snow at night in order to reach the Austrian border. Many others would see the same images via Pathé news on their weekly trip to the cinema.

The prime minister and Archbishop of Canterbury spoke out in favour of the uprising and condemned its suppression. The same shock engendered by these images changed the minds too of many previously in support of the Soviet Union. Prominent members of the Labour Party condemned their actions and there were mass resignations from the British Communist Party. There were protests across university campuses and outrage amongst trade union members with dockers refusing to handle Russian ships.

On 21 January 1957, Secretary of State, Rab Butler, a long-standing Conservative politician, gave a formal welcome to the refugees, an accolade rarely given in these circumstances.

This sympathy led to generous donations. In the first two weeks, the British Council for Aid to Refugees (BCAR) received 10,000 letters from households and organisations offering accommodation.[2] Clothing, bedding and household goods worth then £650,000 (now worth £14 million) were donated and the lord mayor's appeal collected £2.5 million in a couple of weeks. The Women's Royal Voluntary Service (WRVS) collected and distributed large volumes of clothing across the country.

Showbusiness leaders set to, organising a large fundraising concert. A prominent photo in the *News Chronicle* showed an old Hungarian man captioned as: 'Once he was somebody, now he's just a refugee.'

If people opened their own homes, support was available including payments under the National Assistance Act.

Some young people children aged 14 and 15 managed to escape and arrive in Britain alone, and were referred to as 'unaccompanied'. National Assistance was not available to anyone under 16 years of age and so child refugees were referred to church or voluntary organisations.

There was no process for checking the accommodation for suitability but the guidance was to pay particular attention where girls under 18 were being placed.

As people began to settle and form roots, BCAR was able to give grants towards house purchases. A sum of £250 was available for those with families. The refugees had to find the property and check what mortgage was available.

Employment was actively sought for arriving refugees although it was recognised that most refugees were not job-ready immediately. Language classes were arranged and it was felt that the refugees could not take up work until they were settled and rested. Language classes could be held up as the same interpreters were needed to work with police registration.

There were jobs available in various parts of the country, including South Yorkshire, Nottinghamshire, Bedfordshire, the Home Counties and London itself. Attitudes were generally positive. Cranes Ltd, an engineering firm, had experience of employing other central Europeans and said they would be willing to consider them for work at their foundry in Ipswich. Interestingly a large number of vacancies were offered in Plymouth; the firm Telecalmet offered 50 vacancies for skilled men and Berketex, the women's clothing maker, offered 150 jobs for female machinists on their extensive production line in December 1956. This reflected the beginning of a move against the austerity of the war years and the managing director saw the chance to employ women staff to make the new fashions.

Accommodation was sourced in the areas where work was available. Individual homes were offered but also hostels needed to be used. In the south-west, the Salvation Army in Plymouth and the YWCA in Penzance were put into operation. Astor Hall, also in Plymouth (and now a care home), acted as both living accommodation and a popular social centre for Hungarians.[3] Army barracks at Dover and Farnborough were also called into use.

There were 500 students from Hungary whose needs were considered.[4] It was estimated that it would take six months of language tuition to be ready to become a student here. Since there was no money available to support these students, sandwich courses were recommended. It was also acknowledged that it was difficult to assess the refugee students' level of attainment. However, funding for a couple of medical students was considered.

A not-insignificant factor in the welcome that the West gave was that the Hungarian refugees were the first to arrive after the establishment of the 1951 United Nations Refugee Convention. By 21 November, 60,000 had come through Austria and within a week the total had risen to 92,000. This gave the United Nations High Commissioner for Refugees (UNHCR) strong leverage to ensure Western governments were willing and able to share the burden of looking after the refugees. Britain's reputation was already tarnished by its role in the Suez crisis and the country was pressed into taking 20,000 Hungarian refugees. In total, thirty-seven countries took in refugees from Hungary. In the first ten weeks of the crisis, the UNHCR coordinated the resettlement of 100,000. Using the 1951 Convention they deemed this group of peoples seeking asylum en-masse as refugees rather than forcing them to go through thousands of individual asylum claims. In total 200,000 Hungarian refugees fled their homeland.

The following are two personal accounts of the uprising.

The first is from the BBC broadcast on 23 October 2006, the fiftieth anniversary of the uprising.

Tom Leimdorfer was 14 years old and living with his mother in the centre of Budapest.[5]
Her parents had both perished in the gas chambers at Auschwitz and Tom's father had died in a prisoner of war camp in Russia. As a small child in Nazi-occupied Budapest his mother sought to hide him. Her situation was slightly easier than others as she was blonde and did not look Jewish.

The uprising towards the end of October started as we have seen with a student demonstration demanding reform and an end to Soviet domination. It escalated rapidly and within days it had been brutally crushed.

From their flat they could see bullet holes and the dead bodies of protestors opposite. A few days later, venturing outside gingerly, Tom saw a tank coming along the road which fired a volley of shots. His mother decided it was time for them to go!

They joined a flood of refugees heading for the Austrian border. Tom was old enough to know he might never see his home again and he packed his button football game. This game was similar to table football and was very popular in Hungary then.

It is something he has kept all these years in England. They boarded a train almost to the border on the pretext of taking a holiday. Detained briefly, they managed to persuade the captors to let them go and were lucky enough to find a man in the village near to the border who was happy to show them the escape route. On the night they escaped, the sky was full of stars and the sky was cloudless. The border post had a revolving light and as it illuminated the sky they all had to duck. But they had a guide who knew where the barbed wire was weak and not electrified and they were able to crawl underneath.

They arrived in Andau, Austria from where they spent some time in a refugee camp before arriving in London on 16 December. Tom joined the local boys' grammar then called Tollington School.

A further tragedy awaited him as his mother, his only relative, died on 11 April 1957. Of course, his personal life changed irrevocably then. At school he studied hard and was admitted to University College, London where he graduated with a first-class honours in Physics. He became a teacher and ultimately a head teacher. It was during this period he met and married his first wife Valerie with whom he had three children. Together they moved to North Somerset where tragedy struck again when Valerie developed a brain tumour. In Somerset he became involved in work with the Society of Friends and worked in areas of ethnic conflict such as Croatia and the former Soviet Union.

He believes his involvement with the Society of Friends and later as a local councillor stem from his time as a young refugee. He remembers what was given to him in Britain and has wanted to give something back. He has always been a Green Councillor in the area and has always sought to right wrongs.

The following is a transcript of an interview the author undertook with Ildiko McIndoe, whose birth-name was, in Hungarian, Ildiko Homolya in May 2019:

Q. I'm assuming that your parents were the refugees from Hungary and you travelled with them to the UK?

A. My mum divorced my father before the Uprising and she only travelled with me to the UK.

Q. What were your parents doing in Hungary? Were they students or workers?

A. Both of my parents worked in a factory, I have no idea what sort. My grandfather, on my mother's side, was a tailor. My grandmother worked at a factory until she retired.

Q. Were they in Budapest when the Russian tanks came, or somewhere else?

A. Yes, Mum didn't leave until after the tanks and the fighting. She was to meet up with some friends and didn't want my father to raise me as he had a new girlfriend, who she didn't like.

Q. How did they manage to escape and how did they travel to England?

A. Hundreds of thousands of refugees caught trains to the various known areas where the fencing had been torn down. She had to pay to get into Austria where we then spent a few months in a refugee camp before being given the option to go to Canada, US, Australia or England.

Q. Were you welcomed on arrival?

A. If you mean to England I think so. I still have an alien registration card which specifies a scar on my chin as identification. The WRVS took care of us. We were originally despatched to disused army barracks in Cannock Chase, Hednesford. My mother worked in the canteen there and I was looked after by other Hungarians in an area for other children.

Q. Did they have temporary accommodation to begin with?

A. After Hednesford we were then moved to Carpenter Road in Edgbaston, Birmingham through the WRVS. We were given clothes, knitted blankets etc. We were then moved again to Park

Road in Sparkhill, Birmingham along with other Hungarian refugees in a three-storey house. We had a living room and a bedroom, shared kitchen with two other families and a shared bathroom with four families, varying in ages. There were some other Hungarians in a house further down the road. The WRVS found my mother work at the British Small Ammunitions Factory in Small Heath, I think it was.

Q. Where did they go to live after that?

A. We moved to Woodlands Road around the corner when I was about 7. I went to the local Catholic School not far away. We managed to buy the house by loaning money off friends.

Q. Did they have help to settle in?

A. I remember the WRVS lady still coming to visit when we moved, so yes they did.

Q. Were there English classes for everybody?

A. No, there were no English classes for anybody. I taught my mum English after I finished school. Everything I learned I passed on.

Q. What was the local community like? And was it welcoming?

A. This is a difficult one. It is hard for me to be negative as I am, by nature a positive person, but there was a lot of discrimination in the 1950s in England. Against the Irish coming over to build roads, the Windrush immigrants around 1948 and continuing, the Polish refugees had already established themselves since the 1940s. Especially in the Midlands, so the Hungarians were late arrivals and not really welcomed with open arms as we would have stood out quite significantly with our foreign language and accents. Not many Hungarians would be able to speak English as the language of choice in schools was German and then later Russian. English as a language subject in school would have been in the 1970s or later. I remember being discriminated against by my teachers and the headmaster, not by my fellow pupils though, we had a laugh.

Q. Was it the same place where you grew up?

A. Yes, we stayed in the general Sparkhill/Moseley area. Though I was transferred to a convent in Edgbaston when I was about 8 then went to grammar school in another part of Birmingham until I went to college. But all schools were around Birmingham.

Q. Did they take on British nationality early on?

A. I do have the nationality papers and I know that they were issued quite early on, in 1960 I believe. I was automatically 'naturalised' as a British national.

Q. Did you ever return to Hungary later on for visits?

A. Up until early 1970 there were many disappearances of people who had taken part in the Uprising, mainly men, who did return and were never seen again. The Russians didn't leave Hungary until early 1990 I believe. You should go to the House of Terror in Budapest, a gruesome place where citizens were tortured and hung! My mother emigrated to Australia in 1973 as a '£10 Pom', with my sister and my stepfather, to be with her close friend who had emigrated a year or so before. The next time I saw my mother was when I was 32 and we all visited Hungary. This was the first time I had met my father since we left.

Q. Anything else you want to add or I've missed?

A. Only that I am also writing a book and I am about halfway through it, about my mother and me. I will keep you posted.

Ildiko then explained further how she had arrived in England as a 3-year-old, unable to speak English and entering a culture which was completely alien to her. Now, as Ildiko McIndoe, an adult, and after a varied career, she has most recently worked as an ESOL (English as a Second Language) tutor in Devon.

She has taught many young students from Spain, France, Germany, Italy, and Hungary! And this is her philosophy: opportunities introduce themselves which enable you to repay, in the main, the kindness and support extended by many people, most of whom Ildiko never met when arriving in England as a refugee more than sixty years ago.

Chapter 13

The Ugandan Asians

U ganda was one of many African countries that became independent from Britain in the 1960s. Apollo Milton Obote became the first prime minister of this newly established republic having been a key player in the independence movement. Challenged by parliament, Obote suspended the constitution and elevated himself to president in 1966. But while he was at the Commonwealth leaders' conference in Singapore in January 1971 he was overthrown by Idi Amin, a general in the Ugandan army and one-time close associate of Obote.

Like other former British colonies, workers had been imported from India in the form of indentured labour in the nineteenth century. In Uganda their job primarily had been to help build the railways. By 1972, the Ugandan Asians formed a substantially prosperous part of the community with many running their own businesses.

However, by August 1972, Amin decided that Asians were a detrimental force in Uganda and they should be expelled.[1] He said that they were sabotaging Uganda's economy and promoting corruption. He appealed to the African population by saying he wanted to return the country back to them. Many Ugandan Asians had British nationality and it was deemed that they should go to Britain. Amin saw it as some kind of revenge against Britain for not helping him with arms against Tanzania. (Later the Uganda-Tanzania war which raged between 1978 and 1979 would lead to the overthrow of Idi Amin.)

Whatever he gave as his motivation, and many doubted his sanity, the result was the expulsion of 27,000 men, women and children within three months. (The 2006 film *The Last King of Scotland* is the story of Nicholas Garrigan, a young Scottish doctor, who travels to Uganda and becomes the personal physician of President Idi Amin. Although fictional, the film is based on events during Amin's rule, and the title comes from a reporter in a press conference who wishes to verify whether Amin, who was known to adopt fanciful imperial titles for himself, declared himself the King of Scotland.)

The organisation of this expulsion was accelerated in September when Amin implied, in a message to Kurt Waldheim, the United Nations Secretary General, that he was sympathetic to the policy of Hitler against the Jews. It was following this disclosure that the British government arranged an emergency mission to airlift the Ugandan Asian people.

The government established the Uganda Resettlement Board to undertake the work of re-settling the 27,000 refugees: 6,000 were able to go directly to relatives but for the remaining 21,000 accommodation had to be found.[2] The biggest problem for the board was the amount of time in which they had to undertake the work, since the bulk of those 27,000 people arrived between September and November 1972. They arrived in typically British autumnal weather. The first priority was accommodation and the immediate solution was to requisition abandoned or disused military camps. We have seen that a similar solution had been used for Eastern European refugees after the Second World War. But the Asian refugees had been used to temperatures touching 40 degrees Celsius and these camps were located in exposed places, which were usually draughty and difficult to heat. The English winter was soon to arrive and particularly for the vulnerable groups amongst them, of which 30 per cent were children under 16 years old and 5 per cent people aged over 60, it was a difficult time. But people across the UK responded with donations of warm clothing.

The next priority was to find long-term accommodation. Of those who left the reception centres the following year, half had been able to find their own accommodation, which was in addition to the 6,000 who had not required accommodation from the beginning. By 1974, the board had been able to assist 8,429 people move into 1,793 local authority houses and 2,437 people into private accommodation. The policy was to try and achieve dispersal for fear of concentrating people in areas where accommodation and services were in short supply. Coupled with this was the fear of racism against the refugees. Avowedly racist groups such as the National Front had grown in the years following Enoch Powell's 1968 infamous 'Rivers of Blood' speech and it was important that the refugees were not subject to their vitriol. Leicester City Council posted an advert in the *Argus* advising the refugees not to come to Leicester for fear of adverse reactions to their arrival there. Years later this returned to haunt an embarrassed council!

By 1973, the board could report that, though some people had gone to what were considered overcrowded areas, a third had been placed by the board in 400 areas across England, Scotland and Wales where 'they have joined or have formed Asian groups to which other families may eventually be added'.

The board agreed with the government advice that the refugees should be dealt with by the same services that the indigenous population relied on.

There was, however, specialist support in appropriate cases and early on the board established the Uganda Asian Relief Trust. Older people in the centres were found accommodation with families and where possible with those they had made friends with whilst living in the centres. Arrangements were made with social service departments to assess people's needs. A specialist social worker seconded by the Department for Health and Social Security (DHSS) in conjunction with doctors and a disablement resettlement officer, assessed the cases of nine physically or mentally ill people for whom regular accommodation was not considered suitable. Where possible they were placed in the community with Asian families.

For families with four or more children, the board managed to find some properties big enough or to house people in two adjacent properties. For those not eligible for Supplementary Benefit, because they had just started work or had been reliant on relatives, the Relief Trust was able to make small grants of not more than £50. This was for such things as carpeting, curtains, heating, household utensils and the tools of a man's trade. These were items, they reported, 'which people in this country take for granted but these poor people had to leave behind them in Uganda'.

There were two large scale grants which proved the exception but for which it was deemed that there was no alternative. One was for two post-graduate students who fell outside the remit of grants from the Department of Education and Science, and another for a family where deaf children were in need of attending a School for the Deaf. These grants from the Relief Board were largely for those who had moved directly into the community on arrival.

The board also recognised the importance of ongoing support in the community. For the first year they had the ability to pay for extra social workers and community workers and encouraged local authorities and community groups to make use of this facility in pursuit of resettlement. Twenty-three Social Service Departments, of which seven were in London boroughs, three in the Home Counties and thirteen in county boroughs, either recruited workers themselves or arranged for community relations councils to do so. In 1974, the London Council of Social Services recruited a worker with specialist expertise to work for eight months with families recently resettled in London.

Their situation was debated in the House of Lords in early December 1974. There was particular praise for the Women's Royal Voluntary Service (WRVS) but equally there was concern for the lack of housing and financial support. Ninety per cent were eligible for Supplementary Benefit at the same rates as the indigenous population. They were worried about housing since it was reported that fewer homes had been built in that year than since 1963. It was felt the refugees were eligible but that their needs could not be escalated ahead of people already on growing local authority waiting lists. The consequence was that this group of refugees generally obtained poorer quality housing. The same process applied in the private housing sector.

In addition, the WRVS undertook to visit approximately 1,300 families in places which were remote from other places where Ugandan Asian families were living. They reported that most families seemed happy but still needed help with day-to-day issues, including employment and benefits. Specialist workshops were arranged in London, Manchester and Birmingham in July 1973 to educate the refugee population about accessing their rights within the complicated welfare system.

At this stage the board realised that some families were undergoing considerable problems and they attributed some of these to the fact they ignored early advice and were dispersed to areas where there was overcrowding and paucity of services. This had presumably been the result of the natural pull of relatives or that refugees had relocated to an area where they could find existing Ugandan Asian neighbours. However, difficulties arose with finding housing and indeed being exploited by unscrupulous landlords.

The board noted that helping people into employment was easier than sorting out housing, particularly as that would usually involve meeting the needs of whole families, both nuclear and extended. Various schemes were tried to ameliorate the problem. A grant was made to the Coordinating Committee for the Welfare of Evacuees from Uganda from April 1973 for a year. An officer was appointed to Shelter Housing Advice Centre (SHAC) in a project jointly undertaken between Shelter and the Catholic Housing Aid Society to advise the families with the view for them to link with areas where both accommodation and employment was available. A second officer was to be funded by the British Council of Churches. Oxfam granted £5,000 for an allied scheme to help families move out of London.

There was also a scheme specifically in Ealing running for 6 months, advising people about housing and job prospects in other parts of the country.

In conclusion, the board had achieved a great deal in a short space of time in terms of accommodating people who had been so unfairly uprooted and displaced. Not surprisingly there was unease about the difficulties of rehousing from the camps, and fears that people could end up in overcrowded conditions in towns where their relatives were already living. They had been tasked by the government with dispersal but the refugees would see that the support and familiarity provided by their fellow countrymen was compensation in their traumatic situation.

Control over housing matters, whether that be in the public or private sectors, was tenuous, and unlike the British Council for Aid to Refugees (BCAR) at the time of the Hungarian refugees, there was no ability to lend money for house purchase.

It is interesting to note the make-up of the staff and volunteers who assisted the refugees through these difficult times. The resettlement camps were largely run by ex-colonial administrators: some from East Africa and others from a variety of colonial postings. They had the advantage of being practised at large-scale administration but with their experience they tended to see the refugees as colonial 'subjects'. Others were volunteers from a variety of local churches, and those from the nascent race relations industry who would have a more politicised attitude.

Volunteers put in several hours of work and many befriended the refugees. At Houndstone in Somerset, the commander William Pollock Morris described how volunteers were assigned to one family so those kind of personal relationships could be built up. In Tonfanau in North Wales there were fond memories of the work done and many refugees subsequently moved to the nearby town of Tywyn.

But elsewhere things were a little different.[3] The resettlement camp at Greenham Common – a name people will remember from the 1980s when a women's peace camp campaigned against cruise missiles placed there – was run by Brigadier Beyts who was becoming more and more irritated by the role of the volunteers. There had been complaints about the food and someone had spoken to the local press. When a social centre was organised he felt things had gone far enough. The social centre offered facilities for the residents across the whole age range. A canteen was available and open from 10am until 11pm. The facilities were popular with residents who volunteered to help in an activity that gave them a clear role every day. Then a disco was started, popular of course with the young people, but seen by Beyts as causing trouble in the local community. A local resident complained that her daughter was meeting up with a boy from the camp and was neglecting her studies.

Although the social centre was established by a number of volunteers, when matters became more disputed and things came to a head just one person was singled out: Diane Woods. She was a long term and enthusiastic volunteer and was sacked by Beyts, which resulted in having her pass to access the camp withdrawn. A later enquiry exonerated him. Presumably openly criticising the camp brigadier was more difficult than dealing with a volunteer.

Probably long forgotten by most, in 1974 a strike erupted at Imperial Typewriters in Leicester.[4] Arriving in 1972/73 a number of Ugandan Asians had obtained jobs at this factory but it came to light that the Asian workers were being discriminated against. It was much more difficult for them to achieve their bonuses since the targets they were set were higher than their English counterparts – and they were being blocked for promotion. They asked for a dedicated shop steward. These grievances simmered for a while but then came to a head, and on May Day 1974, this group of Asians went on strike, together with workers from three other factories. The strike had little support from the official trade unions but the strikers were active, pulling in support from the local community who assisted on local demonstrations and picket lines. Ultimately, they won their dispute but sadly the management moved production away from Leicester! The experience of solidarity and working together in what was the first largely all-Asian strike built a legacy in the community and provided confidence going forward and inspiration to the group of Asian women who were in dispute at the Grunwick Film Processing Laboratories. That dispute erupted in 1977 and hit national headlines.

Fast forward thirty or forty years and it is widely agreed that the Ugandan Asians who were expelled by Idi Amin have been some of the most successful refugees to enter this country.[5] They arrived in the UK with a high standard of educational attainment from schools which administered strict discipline, and combined this with sheer hard work. They had been living a high quality lifestyle in Uganda and were determined to win that back.

Businessmen such as the late Manubhai Madhvani, who lost all his possessions during the 1972 exodus, built up a global empire with interests in sugar, brewing and tourism worth approximately £160 million.

In Leicester it is estimated that Ugandan Asians have transformed the city and in total have created approximately 30,000 jobs following their arrival. It is here that a Mr Kapasi made his fortune in the affluent suburb of Oadby. After university, he trained as an accountant and set up a financial consultancy business, later serving as head of the powerful Leicester Asian Business Association. He was awarded an OBE in 1997. All of his siblings are successful people owning businesses or holding positions at universities or posts in a London council.

Not all have hit the super-rich lists but many have excelled themselves in other ways. These include distinguished columnist Yasmin Alibhai-Brown, Warwickshire cricketer Asif Din, and Tarique Ghaffur, who left the police service in 2008 when he was in the role as Assistant Commissioner of the Metropolitan Police Force.

Others have undertaken careers in IT, industry, local government, the health service and many have excelled at a running small and medium-sized businesses.

As a sign of how those lives have changed, a debate was held in the House of Commons on 6 December 2012, to celebrate forty years since the arrival of the Ugandan Asian refugees.[6] It was convened by Shailesh Vara, the Conservative MP for North-West Cambridgeshire, himself the son of one of the original refugees.

He started by talking about the history of hostility and the advert sent from Leicester council saying people should not come as there were no jobs for them, referenced earlier in this chapter. He credited the then Prime Minister, Edward Heath, who welcomed the refugees despite the prevailing hostile environment. Jonathan Ashworth, a Labour MP representing the Leicester South constituency, said that the city of Leicester was now a stronger and more vibrant city as a result.

Shailesh Vara contrasted the racist 'Go Home' placards at Heathrow Airport, shown by right-wing protesters on their arrival, with the kindness of ordinary citizens who had offered rooms in their home 'sometimes one for a single person, sometimes more for a family'.

Housing offers were recalled, the small rural area of Pontardawe in west Wales had offered, three houses and Councillor Swift of Peterborough offered fifty houses to people then living at the Torfanu camp in North Wales. This went hand in hand with offers of employment which had to be accepted on taking up the housing. For this Councillor Swift received death threats and needed police protection.

Since that time, Shabbir Damani in Peterborough now runs nine pharmacies employing over 100 full-time staff.

Bob Blackman, Conservative MP for Harrow East, also recalled very positive memories. He was a school student at the time and remembers the new boys arriving. They became friends and he visited their houses. He commented on the wonderfully exotic food. Like so many others, he said it was unusual to meet with a family that did not have a doctor, dentist, lawyer, accountant or other professional in their family.

Himat Lakhani became a social worker in Southwark and between 1974 and 1978 he worked with Ugandan Asian refugees, helping their resettlement. Previously, between 1972 and 1974, he had worked with Ugandan refugees dispersed from the camps.

Showing the distance many of the families had travelled, Dr Whitehead, Scottish National Party MP for Banff in Scotland, spoke of

Vinay Ruparelia, now deceased, who as a pharmacist had also found time to establish a number of charities.

As new arrivals, the refugees had worked in a number of factories: British United Shoe Machinery, Imperial Typewrites, GE and Walkers Crisps.

Chris Williamson, Labour MP for Derby North, summed it up by saying that what could have been a terrible disaster had turned into an amazing success story.

It is worth noting that a debate in the House of Commons celebrating the years of a refugee group, rather than discussing their problems, is of significance.

The following is a personal account from one Ugandan Asian refugee who has remained living in Plymouth in the south-west of England.

The author interviewed Bill Meswania at his restaurant 'Veggie Perrin's' on 8 December 2018. Bill Vallabhdas Meswania has run Veggie Perrin's restaurant in Plymouth for twenty-four years, providing the only Gujarati and South Indian food in Devon. He is well regarded in the community and has involved himself in charitable and fundraising events.

I was 13 years old when I left Uganda. My father had worked as a carpenter for a company called Madwani which refined sugar. Workers had rented accommodation provided by the company according to their grade. Ours was a two-bedroomed semi-detached house in a row with others. They constituted Indian Workers' quarters. As children we played in the front of the house: it was always hot, approaching and sometimes exceeding 40 degrees Celsius.

We were living in the township of Takire, just outside Jinger: that's on the Nile near Kampala. The capital, Takire, had been built and run by the Madwani Company. It was a large area, approximating to the geographical size of Dartmoor, South Devon.

My parents originally came from India and my brothers and sisters had all been born in Kenya. The family had been living in Uganda for eleven or twelve years before Idi Amin came to power. Amin didn't like all the successful commerce being in predominantly

Asian hands. It was said Amin had had a dream in which Allah told him that Asians were dominating everything in the country and they must leave. I remember playing cricket at school when I was first told of all this. Amin nationalised all the companies and told Asian residents they had ninety days to leave with all their possessions!

The access roads to the airport were guarded by conscript soldiers who were largely uneducated. People were afraid. There were rumours that the soldiers would kidnap young women and sexually assault them. It was unpredictable: sometimes people might greet the soldiers and be ignored but sometimes the soldiers would rifle butt them. It was very chaotic when they had to leave. We could take only £55 sterling in foreign currency and were allowed a maximum of 23kg of hold luggage on plane. My parents ended up sending clothing and other possessions to relatives in India. I remember being told that the Madwani Company did assist this emergency exodus by organising buses for their workers to travel to the airport.

There were lots of checkpoints on the way to the airport at Entebbe. Luggage was routinely looted and there was the ongoing fear that women and girls in the group might be taken way and raped.

The soldiers searched everything. I remember that some Asian guys had beer in their bus: some was given to the soldiers as a bit of a bribe and to calm them down. But people were always on edge as they feared trigger-happy soldiers.

My family amongst the other deportees had to pay for their own flight. Amin had frozen their assets. My older brother, Eddie, went with Dad to the High Commission to sort this out. We were only allowed to take 100,000 shillings in the local Ugandan currency which is equivalent to between £25,000 and £50,000 sterling.

We arrived in England on October 15th at night. At the airport we were given tea to drink with rich tea biscuits! We were allocated to a coach which would took us all the way to Plaisterdown Camp on Dartmoor near to Tavistock. On the journey I remember that we were accompanied by volunteers from the St John Ambulance Brigade. The route took us down along the A303 (before the M5 and A38 were built) and at some point during the night I remember stopping at a café where they had some food and some of the guys in my group flirted a bit with the staff. We eventually reached Plaisterdown, which was an ex-military camp, at five o'clock in the morning. My family was allocated to a dormitory first, which was on the outside of the building and therefore very cold and windy. They were welcomed by the WRVS and all of them had to have an X-ray. We stayed at Plaisterdown for three weeks. I have some memories of the time: as kids it still felt like an adventure. We had our first English curry which was rather different from ones at home and we did have some English language lessons. We all disliked the maths teacher! However, I joined the Red Cross at this time.

They closed Plaisterdown Camp after three weeks and people were transferred to the Honiton Camp but by that time my father was given a job as a carpenter at Fitzroy Joinery on Valletort Road in Plymouth. We then rented a house at 41, Valletort Road, a significant milestone.

I remember that my sister and I undertook an educational attainment test at Plymouth Civic Centre. Following that we were allocated to Penlee Secondary School which then became Stoke Damerel Comprehensive, later Stoke Damerel Community College. After our GCSEs I was transferred to Devonport High School for Boys, while my sister obtained employment at the Toshiba plant, then a major employer in Plymouth. All of the younger family were in Plymouth but my older sister and brother had left Uganda for India and it was a big struggle to sort out their entry to England in order that our family could be reunited.

One local woman I remember who helped the family was Mrs Wells, a neighbour, who helped us light fires with firelighters, a novelty for us. Cold was a constant problem and so we pushed our beds together for warmth at night.

I remember that a social worker from the council came to visit us to ensure that we were ok and she asked if we were experiencing any problems at school. However she found my real name, Vallabhdas, difficult to pronounce so she asked me what my mum called me, which was Valam. She decided, however, to call me the nearest English phonetic equivalent she could think of, which was William and over time that became the name I am now called by, which is Bill.

In the early 1970s, attempts to pronounce non-English names correctly were not very successful; Plymouth had virtually no non-white inhabitants. Bill says racism was not overt but it was constantly present.

'For example, people would ask me whether my family would be going back after the fall of Idi Amin, ignoring the fact our family had now made a new home here and we all had British passports.'

They were the only people of colour. 'I remember being called a Paki on the street which perplexed me, knowing that I was not from Pakistan'.

Interestingly, Bill had a really good friend called Michael and they joked about some racist insults. 'One day he called me a "blackie" near to the Plymouth pannier market in town. A policeman overheard this exchange and gave Michael a lecture about his racist remarks. This would have occurred sometime in the late 1970s.' Bill had to intervene to help his friend out.

Seventeen Ugandan Asian families arrived in Plymouth from the Plaisterdown camp but after ten years they had all left to move elsewhere in the UK. Bill's family is the last surviving unit.

I recall that at school there was little interest expressed, either from teachers or other pupils in my family or our life in Uganda or how they came to be England. Some neighbours and like-minded people in Plymouth were interested to talk to us about our story but most people were indifferent.

I was once called n-----r on the street but I thought it was simply the response of an uneducated person with no idea since the term refers to being a black man, African or Caribbean.

Many of the people he came with have moved on. Some are in East London, a friend from his school in Uganda is now settled in Solihull. There are very occasional 'get togethers' from the original camp. Interestingly his nephew, working in Leicestershire, met some IT/computer people from Plymouth doing a presentation who were surprised he had heard of and knew Plymouth, until he mentioned Veggie Perrin's restaurant, at which point there was a slight astonishment as well as mirth.

After going to Plymouth Polytechnic, where I undertook a Higher National Diploma in mechanical engineering, I went to work for two years at Toshiba where now both my brother and sister were working. I wasn't keen on entering into the corporate world and around that time I did some work as a waiter at the Taj Mahal restaurant, in Plymouth. I felt that the food provided wasn't authentic Indian food so, after a spell working with double glazing with a friend, I started to think about opening my own restaurant serving authentic Indian food. There then arose a time-gap when we were fighting to bring our sister over from India, which involved an expensive and protracted battle with the Home Office and the challenge of paying for the lawyers. However, in 1995 I finally succeeded in opening my vegetarian Indian restaurant, Veggie Perrin's. The idea for the name was jointly conceived with good my friend, John McKnight, from the *Western Morning News*. As fans of the 1970's sitcom 'Reggie Perrin' we took the classic saying of the boss CJ 'I didn't get where I am today by—' which they turned into 'I didn't get where I am today by eating meat' and substituted Veggie for Reggie. A perfect name for a great vegetarian restaurant!

My father died aged 90 just before Christmas 2018 and my mum is looked after permanently by my brother Eddie and his wife.

Bill's restaurant and the food he creates for events for charities and other community functions have made a distinct difference to the culture of Plymouth. The city has progressed from the 1970s when Bill first arrived here and has become more diverse and culturally aware. However, there is still a long way to go to be able to compare it with a larger city such as Leicester where friends and relatives of Bill's live.

Chapter 14

The Chilean Coup and its Aftermath

On 11 September 1973, the democratically elected socialist government of President Salvador Allende of Chile was overthrown by General Pinochet and his military forces, with the help of the CIA. Pinochet, determined to stamp out all opposition, began to round up all potential political opponents. Anyone with any connection to left-wing parties were his targets. In the capital, Santiago, people were imprisoned in the national football stadium and from there most were tortured and subsequently murdered.

Terrified, those not yet imprisoned needed to make plans to leave the country. As ever, some people fled across local borders into such countries as Peru and Argentina but many sought refuge in sympathetic countries in Europe.

We have seen that support and sympathy for refugees was predicated on the policies of the receiving country. Under Elizabeth I, the 'Strangers' were welcomed because they were Protestants fleeing an oppressive Catholic rule and because they could bring productive skills to the country. The Jews who had fled Russian pogroms were discriminated against by the xenophobic organisation of the 'British Brothers League' who effectively campaigned for the government to legislate for the Aliens Act of 1905.

With the Poor Palatines we could see they attracted sympathy from the Whigs but opposition from the Tories, whose rise to power in 1709 effectively ended any support they received in Britain.

The comparison is made since the treatment of refugees from Chile followed a not dissimilar path.

The Chilean coup in September 1973 took place when Ted Heath's Conservative government was in power in Britain. The first attempt of refugees from Chile to seek sanctuary in this country involved seven post-graduate students who were associated with Allende's civil service.[1]

Travelling through France, they entered Britain and at the port of entry immigration office, declared themselves as visitors. As such they were treated by the officials as ordinary applicants with limited leave to remain. However, they had left a murderous regime which they could not rely on to ensure their safety if they returned, especially because of their association with the former President Allende. It is worth stating that the fact of claiming asylum, therefore criticising their home country, represents an increased risk of harm for those people if they return.

The case of these seven students became, to an extent, a 'cause célèbre'. Having arrived as visitors, the immigration officer treated them under the rules providing them with limited leave. On their behalf it was pointed out that they could not possibly be expected to return within a year, in view of the turbulent and hostile situation in Chile. By the end of 1973, as many as 10,000 people had been killed by the regime.

Debate concerning the situation in Chile had already reached parliament when, on 4 December, the government was asked why people could not seek sanctuary in the British Embassy in Santiago, the Chilean capital city. The government responded that it was against the principle of diplomatic relations and people would only be offered sanctuary in extreme circumstances where, for example, mob rule prevailed. There were many people in Chile seeking sanctuary at this time because of the actions of the Pinochet government.

Maybe the government's response was due to a fear concerning the numbers of potential Chileans who would be seeking asylum or alternatively because the British government was in the process of recognising the new Chilean regime. The parliamentary opposition pointed out that many other countries' embassies had already offered sanctuary with no repercussions.

As it transpired, their case was taken up by the NUS (National Union of Students) National Secretary, Steve Parry, and it is notable that many academics, aware of the treatment of people in Chile, advocated strongly in support of the Chilean refugees. In November 1973, a Conservative MP, Harold Soref, a leading member of the Conservative Monday Club, objected to help being offered to Chileans alleging 'they are Marxists'. This was, however, rebutted by many members of the public.

On 20 December that year, the case was taken up by Judith Hart, a Labour MP, and was reported in Hansard. She asked that the Home Secretary, Robert Carr, exercise discretion and argued that, whilst they had entered as visitors, given the circumstances in Chile that they be treated as refugees. Robert Carr said that the case would be looked at again but he was minded that they should still be treated under the rules for visitors. One MP, John Wilkinson, implied that the Labour Party wanted the rules bent in favour of its own views. Clinton Davis, MP for Hackney, wanted to be sure that the Home Secretary had not been approached by the Chilean government to refuse them entry here. This was of concern because the British government had just recognised the Military Junta. The Home Secretary denied that this was the case.

The following February, 1974, the Labour government of Harold Wilson came to power. The case of the Chilean students came to the attention of Alex Lyon, Immigration Minister.

By this time the group of Chilean refugees had reduced to four, since three of the students had been given admission as refugees to Norway.

On 26 March, Mr Lyon said: 'I can see no reason for continuing to refuse to allow the remaining four to come in for settlement; in practical terms they are refugees and I am not concerned at the technicalities.' He instructed his staff to ring their solicitors 'before we make the letter public'. It was thus that the political mood had changed in favour of recognising the rights of those seeking asylum under the 1951 UN convention.[2]

The groundwork for the reception of Chilean refugees following the military coup was done by the Chile Committee for Human Rights, the Chile Solidarity Campaign and the Joint Working Group for the Resettlement of Refugees from Chile (JWG) in the UK and Academics for Chile (AFC). A huge amount of lobbying was done on the basis of the information collected mostly from the *Comité Pro Paz* (Committee for Peace, later the *Vicaría de la Solidaridad* (Vicariate of Solidarity)) set up by the churches in Santiago.

The coordination of help and support was provided by charities.[3] Initially, the British Council for Aid to Refugees (BCAR) took up the role receiving 100 refugees. The Joint Council for Refugees of Chile was established at this point and they worked with the government and

Christian Aid. As we have seen academics were active in their support for Chilean refugees and the World University Service collaborated with other groups to support the refugees. These groups included Chile Solidarity Committee, Chile Committee for Human Rights and Academics for Chile. The World University Service Programme (WUS) alone granted scholarships to 900 refugees, whose studies had been interrupted, to come to this country. In all, around 2,500 Chilean refugees came to Britain.

Within a year or so, Pinochet started offering visas to political prisoners enabling them to leave the country. He saw this as part of his strategy to rid the country of all leftists. Many did not want to accept this 'offer' seeing this as an expulsion from their own country. On the other hand, if they refused they were told that they could be taken to the Argentine border 'where a lot of things happen'. Since the prisoners had little contact with the outside world it was usually the relatives who arranged for such visas. An English woman civil servant was despatched by the British government to Chile to interview people or their relatives to see if they qualified for what was effectively an exit visa.

It is worth mentioning that in terms of financial support the refugees would have been eligible to claim Supplementary Benefit just as the Ugandan Asians had been. Supplementary Benefit was available to those either with no financial support, income or very little of their own finances. Essentially it acted as a supplement to any significantly low income. Even when this changed to Income Support in 1988, refugees were still able to claim. This ceased in 1996, when the government of John Major abolished the eligibility. In a later chapter we will see how refugees could be, and were, supported following this change.

In the context of Anglo-Chilean relations, which had impacted on decisions whether or not to allow Chilean asylum seekers to enter the UK it should be noted that Pinochet's henchmen were not shy of torturing a British subject. Dr Sheila Cassidy was working out in Santiago and in her work treated an injured revolutionary, Gutierrez. The regime wanted information about the whereabouts of this man and on her refusal to answer them she was tortured in the notorious building the 'Villa Grimaldi'. (That building has now been transformed into the *Parque por la Paz,* which was inaugurated in 1997 as a tribute to those who suffered unthinkable acts at the Villa Grimaldi.)

Whilst imprisoned there, Dr Cassidy also had to witness the torture of young women prisoners. She endured electric shocks and then one day they blindfolded her with tapes to the eyes and she was made to wear sunglasses. In that situation she was marched outside and could hear the sound of an engine revving in front of her, which she believed would run over her. It appeared this terrifying experience was to scare her. She was eventually freed and on her return to Britain she made people aware of what was happening in Chile. Back home, she worked as an oncologist and became well known for her work at St Luke's Hospice in Plymouth.

With fresh reports from Chile coming in repeatedly of torture and killings and the routine rape of women in the national stadium, there was anger and distress here.

As we have seen, in addition to the charities that supported the refugees, organisations were set up to campaign and publicise what was happening in Chile. The most well known of these was the Chile Solidarity Committee (CSC), which continued its work until 1991 when Chile had a democratically elected government once more.[4] This was described by the Peoples' History Museum in Manchester, who hold its archive, as almost certainly the most effective organised opposition outside of Chile itself. The CSC was active in organising lobbies of parliament, directly and through letter, postcard and telegram campaigns. Similarly, the Foreign office and the British and Chilean embassies were lobbied. Leading members of the AUEW (Amalgamated Union of Engineering Workers) and the TGWU (Transport and General Workers' Union) joined the campaign. This included their secretary, Jack Jones, who had himself fought in the Spanish Civil War.

The Parliamentary Labour Party formed a special working group on Chile and in 1981, eighteen Labour Party members of parliament attended a national demonstration for Chile – such was the prominence and revulsion at the events of 1973 and of the Pinochet regime.

Leading politicians such as Judith Hart and Martin Flannery were active members, and actors such as Emma Thompson and Glenda Jackson lent their support.

Birmingham Chile Solidarity campaign has an account online of its campaign, featuring interviews with refugees who arrived in the 1970s and have settled in the area. Margaret Stanton was a founding member and describes the horror they all felt when they heard about what was happening to people in the national stadium in Santiago.[5] She, too, had heard of what happened to Dr Sheila Cassidy.

Pedro, Sergio, Idulia and Apollo were all refugees who had arrived in the UK from 1974 onwards using the visas, already described. Pedro was confused at first when shown a letter about the visa, since in prison he had no contact with officials. He realised that his family had made all the arrangements for him. Idulia, a social worker, didn't want the visa but after the Pinochet regime threatened her daughter she felt she had no choice but to accept it.

When they arrived they stayed initially at a hotel in Shepherd's Bush before moving on. Effectively they were all exiles but they made a life here and were successful. Sergio ultimately became head of the union at GEC in Coventry having worked there for thirty years. All expressed their gratitude for the support that they had received here. Joan Santana is a founder member of the Banner Theatre group which is still thriving and on a personal note she married Apollo. This echoes the author's own experience where, in the 1970s in London, two friends also married Chilean refugees and had families.

There is no doubt that Chilean refugees received a warm welcome here from trade unions, socialist groups and church groups. The 'Chile in Exile' website lists the actions of seamen refusing to sail on ships which were planning to dock at Chilean ports; in Newhaven and Liverpool the dockers refused to unload Chilean goods, and factory workers refused to make spare parts for British Leyland in Chile. These actions were communicated to Chileans at home and helped boost their morale.

Refugees were welcomed across the country by charitable and voluntary groups and they had a particularly strong welcome in Scotland. In Cowdenbeath in Fife, a group arrived and were welcomed by the miners' pipe bands. Cottages had been prepared for their accommodation with warm blankets on the beds since the Scots thought that they might be cold. This level of consideration was much appreciated by the newcomers.

The trade union response in Scotland was resolute.[6] In 1974, aircraft engines sent from Chile to be repaired in Scotland were temporarily confiscated and the employees refused to do work for such a murderous regime. It transpired that these engines had been removed from the aircraft which had been used to bomb the presidential palace the year before when Allende was in residence. Recently (2018) a film, *Nae Pasaran*, reflecting the slogan of republicans in the Spanish Civil War mixed with Scottish slang, has been made about their actions.[7] Movingly it was not until many years later that the workers learnt that their actions had saved the lives of seven prisoners that the Pinochet regime freed because of their actions in Scotland.

From Sergio, who is featured in the account of the Birmingham Chile Solidarity Campaign, there is a moving account of this.

He was being regularly tortured but, taken near the guard's office one day, he heard on the radio a report giving an explanation of the boycott of the Rolls Royce engines in Scotland. He described how he had been near the end of his tether but this news, showing people abroad were fighting for them, gave him great strength and fortitude. It is a wonderful account of solidarity from trade unionists in pushing for change at this terrible point in Chile's history.

Early in 1977, Allende's widow, Hortensia Bussi, spent time in Scotland. She ran for rector of Glasgow University and although she lost the election she was able to raise awareness of what was going on in Chile. The lessons of such solidarity have not been forgotten by those involved.

Chapter 15

A Vietnamese Story

T he Vietnamese peoples have a long history of defensive warfare against foreign occupiers.[1] As long ago as 1418, they fought a guerrilla war against the Chinese for a period of almost ten years. In 1859, the French captured Saigon and by 1859 they had transformed the whole country into a French Protectorate. Resistance to French occupation was continuous until Japan invaded the country in 1940 following the fall of France and its occupation by Hitler's Germany.

Very shortly after the end of the Second World War, the Vietnamese revolutionary leader, Ho Chi Minh, declared independence from French Indo-China, on 2 September 1945, and announced the creation of the Democratic Republic of Vietnam. However, France re-asserted its colonial dominance by re-occupying the country and a war (the First Indo-China War) ensued between France and the Viet Minh, led by President Ho Chi Minh. The Viet Minh ('League for the Independence of Vietnam') was a coalition of nationalist groups, mostly led by communists. In February 1951, the communists announced the creation of the Lao Dong Party (Labour Party), gradually marginalizing non-communists in the mainly agricultural areas. Eventually, following the defeat of France, a Geneva Conference was convened from 26 April–20 July 1954 by the major nations resulting in the Geneva Accords.

It was intended to settle outstanding issues resulting from the Korean War and the First Indo-China War. The part of the conference on the Korean question ended without adopting any declarations or proposals, so is generally considered less relevant. The Geneva Accords that dealt with the dismantling of French Indo-China proved to have long-lasting repercussions, however. The crumbling of the French Empire in south-east Asia would create the eventual states of the Democratic Republic of Vietnam (North Vietnam), the State of Vietnam (the future Republic of Vietnam/South Vietnam), the Kingdom of Cambodia, and the Kingdom of Laos.

For the Indo-China negotiations, the Accords were between France, the Viet Minh, the USSR, the People's Republic of China, the US, the UK and the future states being made from French Indo-China. The agreement temporarily separated Vietnam into two zones, a northern zone to be governed by the Viet Minh and a southern zone, split along the seventeenth parallel, to be governed by the State of Vietnam, then headed by former emperor Bao Dai.

A truce between the Communist North and South Vietnam, supported by their American allies simmered for some time. America had always kept advisers in South Vietnam but when one of their ships was attacked off the coast in 1964 it began to introduce new reinforcements of troops. By December 1965, there were 183,000 American servicemen and by the following year numbers had risen to half a million. The inevitable war that ensued was known as the Second Indo-China war as well as (in Vietnam) the Resistance War against America. But to those living in the West it was simply known as the Vietnam War.

It was a very bitterly fought conflict, resulting in many deaths but also terrible injuries from the use of chemical agents, such as Agent Orange, by the American military. It was not until April 1975 that the Americans finally withdrew. The photo of an American helicopter leaving the rooftop of their embassy in Saigon with Vietnamese supporters desperately hanging on to the struts provides one of the most graphic images of the twentieth century.

The Hanoi government of the north took over the whole country after the South Vietnamese government collapsed. People who had worked with the Americans and the South Vietnamese government were fearful of reprisals and looked to escape from the country.

In those early days, few refugees came to Britain, most opting to seek refuge in the US, France and Australia. In 1975, only 300 were given leave to remain here. It was not until the late 1970's border disputes with China and their subsequent invasion of Vietnam that Chinese Vietnamese citizens, mainly from Northern Vietnam, began to flee. They were losing their properties and jobs in a government-sponsored campaign to force them out of the country.

Many of these people fled to Hong Kong and from there hoped to reach America. Initially, escaping by plane was impossible; consequently people took to boats. Given the pressures to get away, many boats were dangerously overcrowded. They were reminiscent of the boats carrying the Basque children and currently those crossing the Mediterranean. The boats were attacked by pirates, people were killed or otherwise sold into slavery. The seas they were travelling across were also notoriously shark-infested.

The numbers of people increased and by September 1978, a veritable exodus ensued. Not knowing what to do, the Indonesian government unloaded a boat on an uninhabited island. Another boat attempted to do the same thing with 2,500 people on Malaysian shores and thousands attempted to land in Hong Kong. As a geographically dense area, Hong Kong became a place of asylum and transit where applications were made for the refugees to be passed onto receiving countries. The demands for rescue and essential assistance far-outstripped the resources allocated by the contiguous countries.

The international response was also slow. Thus, in 1979 there were 3,200 people in the camps in Hong Kong.

It was clear that some alternative, internationally coordinated action needed to be undertaken and thus a conference was called to pull together these disparate efforts.[2] As the newly elected prime minister of the UK, it was Margaret Thatcher's first international negotiation. Initially she favoured funding pre-fabricated homes in the Far East over providing safe homes for refugees. However, as negotiations progressed she asked what the naval fleets of other countries would do and stated that Britain had no automatic duty to take refugees from those boats and ships.

Nevertheless, ultimately Britain did accept quite large numbers of the Vietnamese refugees when eventually Margaret Thatcher agreed, reluctantly, to the UK accepting them. In the first place 1,500 Vietnamese refugees were taken in, followed by a further 14,000.

There was also a mission specifically aimed at rescuing Vietnamese children who had been assumed to be orphans by the *Daily Mail* newspaper. These children had been living in appalling conditions in the camps and sadly soon after arrival three of them died.

Some other children, who had been assumed to be orphans turned out to have their own parents. A court case then ensued with the Ockenden Venture, a national charity who had care of these children, contesting custody and challenging the return of some children to their parents. This action succeeded. It is a sad feature of attempts to help vulnerable children in war situations that their rights may be overlooked.

Given the vast distances involved, those refugees accepted by the government, were flown by charter flights directly to Britain.

Once the refugees arrived in Britain, primarily from the temporary camps in Hong Kong, help was on offer from three different agencies:

1) British Council for Aid to Refugees
2) The Ockenden Venture and
3) Save the Children Fund

All operated their own reception procedures but were coordinated by the Joint Committee for Refugees from Vietnam usually referred to as 'the Secretariat'.

On arrival, the refugees were referred to a reception centre which undertook the following functions:

1) Complete medical checks.
2) Provision of English Language courses.
3) Help to orientate to a British way of life.
4) To formulate a resettlement programme – including reports on family and medical backgrounds, educational needs, employment skills and special consideration regarding accommodation.
5) Resettlement. Housing offers nationally were coordinated by the Secretariat which had been set up by the Home Office in October 1979. Detailed negotiations were conducted for the Ockenden Venture by the lettings coordinator who was based at their Birmingham Unit.
6) Support groups.

The charities sought assistance from a variety of community organisations, such as the Council for Voluntary service, church groups, the Round Table and the Lions Club. The Secretariat liaised with statutory agencies in the form of housing, employment and education.

The desire was to resettle family groups within a short distance of each other in order to facilitate support. However, given the poor spread of council housing this could rarely be achieved.

The problem of re-housing was not straightforward.[3] Those working in the statutory sector had additional problems at this time. Legislation allowing for the sale of council housing was introduced in the autumn of 1980. As public housing was sold off and not replaced, this decreased the overall stock. Shortly after this the London housing authority under the auspices of the Greater London Council, the GLC, started to shed its housing and return these back to the individual London boroughs. Generally speaking, this meant only those local councils had the right to allocate and therefore mobility was restricted. However, what was deemed 'hard to let' property might be allocated to groups such as refugees. Allocations already made could put a lone Vietnamese family in a place far from friends and relatives. When the author was working in Greenwich in the 1980s one Vietnamese family had been placed on the Ferrier Estate, an isolated 1960's council estate in south-east London with few facilities, and where the rest of the population was white working class.

The GLC also had the job of trying to persuade housing authorities across the country to offer up accommodation. It was felt that none were very keen but one stuck out: Plymouth, of which it was said 'nothing arranged, very unlikely to agree!'

In 2007, a report by the Runneymede Trust looked at the lives and experiences of the Vietnamese refugees since their arrival.[4] It touched on the dispersal policy, which it said was primarily designed to lessen the burden of cost of the care and integration on receiving local authorities and charities.

Alongside this it sought to forestall any 'ghettoisation' of the refugees clustering in one place. However, through lack of support networks in the communities to which people were dispersed, people became isolated. Not surprisingly the refugees began to 'vote with their feet' and go to areas where Vietnamese had formed communities and where support with jobs and accommodation was likely. Populations in London, Birmingham and Manchester increased at this time, alongside the process of family reunification.

Estimates at the time of the report show at least 22,000 living in England with 60 per cent of that total living in London. Most were in the South London boroughs of Lambeth, Southwark and Lewisham, which had its own translation service.. Among the early refugees it is known that at least 76 per cent had received education below secondary school level. Not surprisingly, parents were keen for their children to make best use of their education in England – which wasn't available in their country of origin. Interestingly, in Lambeth, London exam results in 2000 show that girls far out-performed the boys; 67 per cent of girls achieved five or more GCSEs at A to C grades compared with only 10 per cent of boys.

Employment

Vietnamese refugees found difficulty entering the workplace particularly those who, through dispersal, had been sent to places of high unemployment. Their lack of English skills contributed to this problem. Most were from the north where educational opportunities had been limited; their neighbours from the south were far more advantaged. In addition to this, most had farming and fishing skills which could not easily be adapted to their new environment. In the UK, work available to refugees initially was in the catering business followed by the garment industry. In recent years, Vietnamese entrepreneurs have entered the nail bar industry in a major way.

Language fluency remains a barrier. Indeed, many of the refugees were not literate in their own language. Children had to act as translators in delicate matters such as health. Lack of language meant they would either seek help within their community or leave it: being too intimidated to call services. The Lewisham PCT (a translation service) has reported that of the 130 languages available, the highest call for interpretation was for Vietnamese. Lack of confidence and shyness also provided a block to accessing services they were entitled to use.

The following account is by Julia Meiklejohn who worked with the organisation Save the Children Fund as one of the three groups ensuring reception and settlement of Vietnamese refugees starting in 1979:

Early Work with Refugees (Save the Children & Refugee Action):
August 2018
Julia Meiklejohn
Save the Children Fund[5]

I started work in July 1979, just after Save the Children Fund was asked to deliver part of the programme for refugees from Vietnam. I understand Save the Children Fund was brought into the programme, with a director who was a senior social worker, to balance BCAR and the Ockenden Venture who were perceived as having different methods of working. At that time there were refugees who had been rescued by British-registered boats and that summer there the British Government was 'persuaded' to make a commitment to refugees in Hong Kong camps as other countries said they would not take people from Hong Kong without British involvement.

The culture within the British refugee sector was what I can only described as neo-colonial so we felt that this was not acceptable. In terms of innovation:

- Firstly, we appointed a project leader to manage reception in group interviews which looked for people who could listen and lead a team with respect. The project leaders then appointed their own teams including a nurse, a translator and settlement workers. At that time the local authorities were tasked with language teaching which happened within centre.
- The reception centres were to be medium size – big enough for a full team of workers but small enough for refugees to have some control over their lives. We found buildings for peppercorn rents which authorities were not using at the time but wanted to retain long term. These were from local councils, health authorities and the like. We felt BCAR centres were too big and thus institutional and those of the Ockenden Venture too small for a full complement of staff.
- Each centre operated its own programme within bounds and project leaders met regularly to share ideas and problems. Settlement was mostly local but refugees were usually given information that would help them move later. Dispersal was

government policy but we always thought that people needed support from their own community and many of the Vietnamese had to move from original settlement areas.

- At one of our project leader meetings, two workers, (one a Vietnamese social worker and the other a Kenyan Asian social worker), pointed out that translators were actually doing most of the advice work and understood the needs of their community. Unofficially we persuaded the Home Office to allow us to train Vietnamese translators as para-social workers. We were thinking of longer-term resettlement work as well as reception work. We continued to pay the translators as translators and used spare capacity in one of the reception centres. It was becoming obvious that work was going to be needed well after reception especially with a group who came from a non-European background and with some not literate even in their mother tongue.

- We set up a school in one reception centre to fulfil a need we had identified among older teenagers who had missed out on vital years at school but clearly had the ability to move onto university/college. The children were there for two years and learned very quickly with qualified staff, some with Vietnamese/ Chinese language skills. Save the Children Fund financially supported this.

- We set up a reception centre for unaccompanied minors as adoption was not appropriate for children who had relatives in their home country or other resettlement countries. Many were later reunited with families. Save the Children Fund continued with this project.

- As the quota was nearing completion and reception centres closing, we approached Save the Children Fund in terms of the need for a longer-term programme. They agreed to continue with programmes for children but felt the other work was not within their brief.

- Save the Children Fund helped us set up a new charity – Refugee Action. They gave a small amount of legal advice and we were able, through senior staff moving over from SCF, to continue contacts and trust. For example, they knew that our budgeting was accurate and not inflated.

Refugee Action

Refugee Action was established in the autumn of 1981 with one member of staff moving immediately from Save the Children Fund and one staying to finish the previous project and move to Refugee Action later.

In terms of innovation:

- One of the cornerstones of Refugee Action was the concept of para-social work. Many of the students became staff members and some went to work with local authorities. We decided to set up community offices in resettlement areas with mixed British Vietnamese/Chinese teams. The central team was to be small.
- Having decided this we looked at the pay issue. Considering qualification/experience it became clear that a pay scale would be British, then Chinese and then Vietnamese. Therefore, we introduced equal pay for all. I organised the budgets based on accepted pay scales and then redistributed the staffing budget fairly. The Home Office knew we were doing this. Equal pay unfortunately ended when I left the CEO's post.
- We decided to base the management team outside of London to make a point that much of the work was regional and to keep costs low. We were first in Leeds and then in Derby. We had access to Rowntree's Social Services Trust shared office in London through our chair Pratap Chitnis.
- When the Vietnamese programme, which included the community work, was running down completely there was an internal debate about whether we should disband. The principle was that the work was more important than the organisation. Refugee Action should only exist if it were doing useful work. It was decided to continue as other refugees' needs were coming to our attention.

  The first was housing issues within the Tamil refugee community.
- In terms of the status of Refugee Action we were not precious about what we did ourselves. We facilitated the setting up of other organisations when we thought this would be more effective. We set up the Refugee Arrivals Project to undertake work at the airports and then assisted the setting up of a new charity. We

realised that the policy and funding framework was different in Scotland so instead of creating Scottish Refugee Action we set up Scottish Refugee Council with some of our staff moving across to this organisation.

I hope that our inheritance is always to put the need of refugees first and to look at the best ways of working, if necessary going against the mainstream consensual thinking. For example, the establishment of the Voluntary Return project. Unfortunately, this became mainstream through Home Office funding and was later changed by the government.

Cambodia, a Tragic Story.

Just as the Vietnam War was ending, its neighbour Cambodia was entering the most traumatic time in its history. On 17 April 1975 a group of Cambodians known as the Khmer Rouge led by Pol Pot marched into the capital Phnom Penh thereby taking over the country. Their philosophy and aim was to bring Cambodia back to 'Year Zero'. To do this they aimed to revert to a peasant society eliminating anything modern and technological. This also meant eliminating middle class and educated people. Some were sent to rural areas to work on the farms but with meagre rations many died of illness and starvation. Others were rounded up and killed by brutal means, usually by having their heads stoved in with cudgels. Children were not exempt from these procedures. The Khmer Rouge photographed all their victims first, obviously happy to use modern technology when it suited them. It is estimated that in just that short space of time from 1975 to end of 1978 between 2 or 3 million Cambodians perished of which 1.7 million were murdered directly.

At the end of 1978, the Vietnamese army swept into Cambodia and overthrew the Khmer Rouge. It was the first time people were really able to escape and refugees poured across the border into camps in neighbouring Thailand.

Ultimately most refugees went to live in the USA. However there is a record in Hansard in January 1980 of 168 Cambodians being admitted to Britain 'most of whom have close relatives here'. Uniting families in times of distress is a needed humanitarian measure.

What happened in Cambodia remains a hidden history for most people.

Chapter 16

The Balkan Wars in the 1990s and the Kosovo Humanitarian Evacuation Programme

During the 1990s, the Balkans, a region in south-eastern Europe, were the scene of some brutal wars.[1] This came about as a result of the disintegration of former Yugoslavia. Yugoslavia was a federated state, formed after the Second World War and consisted of six Republics: Slovenia; Croatia; Serbia; Bosnia and Herzegovina; Montenegro and Macedonia – now known as North Macedonia, and two provinces: Kosovo and Vojvodina. All of these eight constitutional entities enjoyed a fairly comparable and substantial autonomy and federal decision-making power. Ever since the formation of Yugoslavia, there had been tensions between these ethnic groups, especially between Serbs and Croats, the two largest nations. However, these were well contained during the fairly relaxed Communist regime under the long-serving President Tito, who came to power straight after the Second World War.

When Tito died, in 1980, these tensions resurfaced, in particular with a marked rise of nationalism among the Serbs, and this was rapidly intensified and exploited when Slobodan Milošević came to power in the mid-1980s. Milošević started to concentrate the federal power in the hands of Serbia and in doing so, the first step was to abolish Kosovo's autonomy during late 1989 and early 1990. Kosovo was rich in natural resources and its population was mainly Albanian. The Albanians had been historically the most oppressed nation, not least because they were scattered in Kosovo, Serbia proper, Montenegro and Macedonia. Kosovo's Albanian majority rejected this oppressive treatment, to which the Serbian regime responded with brutal force in the shape of 'political differentiation': imprisoning the more prominent public figures, massive dismissal of Albanians from the security, education and social and healthcare system, rendering them jobless and without any support. Having been left with no other options, especially without recourse to any security structures, and with no support within Yugoslavia at the time, the Kosovo Albanian population opted for peaceful resistance under the leadership of Dr Ibrahim Rugova, an award-winning writer, who oversaw the establishment of a parallel state structure including education and healthcare provision. This was funded by a sizeable Kosovo Albanian diaspora. With the Serbian leadership plans now laid bare, the political and constitutional wrangling between Serbia and the other republics began, leading to the gradual but unstoppable and bloody disintegration of Yugoslavia. By the second half of 1991, the then Yugoslav People's Army had been put, directly or indirectly, under the Serbian command, including in Slovenia and Croatia, which led to them both declaring independence in May/June 1991. This sparked a short war in Slovenia but a protracted and bloody war in Croatia, which culminated in that country finally regaining all of its territory by May 1995. Having retreated in Bosnia, from Slovenia and most of Croatia, the Yugoslav army rebranded itself into the Bosnian Serb Army and between 1992 and 1995 was involved in the bloodiest conflict of all, in Bosnia and Herzegovina, resulting in an estimated 100,000 people killed, including those during the infamous Srebrenica massacre: the largest massacre in Europe since the Holocaust, where over 8,000 defenceless Bosnian men and boys were killed within a week or so in July 1995. This massacre took place under what was the assumed protection of Dutch UN troops. Having helped the Serbian army to move the women and children out on buses, 350 men and boys were massacred. Many years later, in 2007, the International Court of Justice ruled the massacre in Srebrenica was genocide.

The Serbian government has never admitted its guilt. More recently, in July 2019, a case in the Dutch Supreme Court found that the Dutch United Nations' soldiers bore 10 per cent culpability. The mothers who travelled to Holland for the verdict felt betrayed.

In the meantime, Macedonia also declared independence, having escaped war because there were only a small number of Serbs living within its borders. By 1996, the new Federal Republic of Yugoslavia, made by Serbia and Montenegro only, recognised Slovenia, Croatia, Bosnia and Herzegovina, and Macedonia.

By late 1997, having experienced multiple wars and international peace conferences, a relative peace was established in most of the former Yugoslavia: peace that most were not happy with, but peace nonetheless.

In Kosovo, however, where it all began, the tensions remained simmering during all this period. Serbia had de facto and de jure taken over Kosovo.

The predominantly young Albanian majority had been growing increasingly frustrated. Whilst the peaceful approach had kept most of the population safe and prevented mass exodus, it had not brought freedom and independence. Early 1998 saw the first armed conflict with disaffected Albanians joining the Kosovo Liberation Army (KLA). The KLA was poorly armed, small in number and was no match for the massive military arsenal that Serbia had by now concentrated in Kosovo, among whom were the notorious paramilitary groups known to have committed atrocities previously in Bosnia. The KLA would sporadically attack military or police personnel to which Serbia would respond with excessive force resulting in mass civil casualties, most notably in the village of Prekaz in March 1998 where fifty-two members of the same family, mostly women and children, were killed.

The international community began to mobilise, and a number of meetings and conferences were held in an attempt to reach a political solution. However, Serbia rejected these attempts. With the conflict escalating, NATO threatened military action should Serbia continue to indiscriminately attack the defenceless civilian population, and it was another massacre in the village of Racak in January 1999 where forty-five villagers were murdered that led to the beginning of NATO aerial bombings on 24 March 1999. It was then that the Serbian state-sponsored, meticulously organised ethnic-cleansing began. With an estimated 1.2 million people on the move – around 800,000 people fleeing or being expelled from Kosovo and 200,000 to 400,000 people internally displaced – the international organisations called this the largest civil population movement in Europe since the Second World War.

Baki's story[2]

At this time, Baki (Baki Ejupi) and Nebi (Nebahate Cakolli), were also on the move, both final year medical faculty students in Prishtina, the capital city of Kosovo. They had been seeing each other for just over three years. They had met up a week prior to the bombing campaign but in the days after they had lost touch. Mobile phones were rare in those days in Kosovo, there were frequent electricity cuts and the Serbian authorities often cut the landlines. Not knowing the whereabouts of each other, all they could do was hope that they were both alive and would be meeting again.

Baki was living in Prishtina with his brother and his family, whereas the rest of his family were in Podujeve, a town in northern Kosovo. It was on the evening of 24 March 1999 that Baki, his brother and his family, like many, many others, were ordered to leave their flat by the Serbian police and paramilitary. They had lost contact with the rest of their family in Podujeve too, among whom were two of Baki's pregnant sisters.

Nebi, on the other hand, was born and lived in another part of Prishtina with her family. Nebi's family was separated in this process as well. Her two brothers were living in London at the time, whereas their father stayed behind 'to keep the fire going'. He was later told by the Serbian paramilitary to 'leave alive or die'. Nebi, her mother and sisters, left together with her mother's side of the family, to be directed towards Macedonia, where she learned that two of her first cousins had been killed by sniper bullets.

Neither Baki nor Nebi wanted to leave Kosovo for many reasons: they knew nothing about what was happening to each other; they didn't know what was happening to the rest of their families, but also because they were close to graduating, realising their dream of becoming doctors and establishing their life together. And so over the next ten days or so they were moved from one part of Prishtina to another, frequently threatened with 'if we see you again, we will kill you', until they finally, together with thousands of other people, were escorted by armed paramilitary, in a convoy, to the city's railway station and put on the train to be taken to neighbouring North Macedonia. They still clearly remember looking through the train windows, they saw soldiers and houses on fire, and, in the midst of the shock, they were thinking this would be the last time they would be seeing Kosovo. It was by chance, or fate that on 3 April 1999 they met, in a place called Blace, no man's land, between Kosovo and northern Macedonia, as the Macedonian authorities initially refused to let refugees in. Eventually, they were allowed into Macedonia and were placed in a temporary refugee camp called Stenkovec, put together by NATO soldiers and various international aid agencies. This is where they started 'living together'.

The idea, and hope, was that after the NATO aerial campaign started, the war would end quickly, and they would go back and carry on with their lives where they had left off. It didn't turn out like that. It was a cold winter, and living conditions were poor, there was no end to the conflict in sight, and more and more people were expelled from Kosovo. There was a growing pressure on the European countries and numerous international aid organisations for a longer-term solution to the escalating humanitarian crisis. As the Kosovo crisis had generated a great deal of interest, twenty-eight countries came forward to take refugees from camps in Albania, Macedonia and Montenegro. It was to be known as the Kosovo Humanitarian Evacuation Programme.

Refugee transfers began in early April. Just over three weeks after they arrived in the camp, Baki and Nebi decided they too should leave, and as Nebi's brothers were in the UK they decided to join them. They were flown to East Midlands airport on 29 April 1999. They, together with another fifty-five refugees, were placed in a reception centre in Stretton, Clay Cross, near Chesterfield. The reception centre was managed by a fantastic charity organisation called Refugee Action, one of the oldest and most experienced charity organisations in the UK working with asylum seekers and refugees. The Refuge Action staff awaited them at the airport, as did a great number of ordinary people from all around Derbyshire, who had been following the events and merely wanted to greet them. They were to stay at the camp for about four and a half months. English and IT classes were provided on site. They received visits from local people, wanting to meet them and offer help in any way they could, some of whom would volunteer to take them on day trips and so on. This was an important and helpful time as it enabled Nebi and Baki to reflect on the events they had been through and recuperate.

On 10 June, the war in Kosovo ended and shortly afterwards they discovered that their family members had survived the war. In September 1999, Nebi and Baki moved into their first, own, family home in Derby. A few weeks later, Baki started working with Refugee Action, the organisation that had supported him in so many ways, as a project worker with the Kosovan Medical Evacuees Project, whereby he supported a small number of children with life-threatening injuries or conditions, who were brought over for treatment in various hospitals in the north-east. Nebi also started working shortly after, as an interpreter and teaching assistant in adult education, supporting Albanian-speaking students.

By September 2000, Nebi and Baki had their first child, Eris, and moved with work to Exeter, where Baki took up a new post as an asylum advice caseworker with Refugee Action. In late 2001, they moved to Plymouth, where Baki took on the role of the deputy office manager for the Devon and Cornwall region. Refugee Action's role was to use its long expertise in working with asylum seekers and refugees to advise and support the new asylum seekers, mainly from the Middle East. They also worked with refugees who had won the right to remain in the UK and assisted them to establish themselves and create their own communities.

Through this work, Baki would liaise closely with the few nascent local refugee organisations. This was in addition to the local authority, for whom this was a new experience and challenge. Among other things, Baki played an important role in establishing the first local translation service in Plymouth called 'Translate Plymouth', which is still functional.

In 2002, in Plymouth, their second child, Hana, was born. Nebi worked part-time and raised their children. It was here where she started to feel increasingly homesick and had some therapy, which enabled her to reflect on her life and to start to make plans for her future as a refugee mother of young children in a foreign country. It was after this experience that Nebi started her training in psychotherapy, which would turn out to be her future career. In 2006, Nebi and Baki returned to Kosovo for a short visit for the first time since being expelled. Baki finished his final exams and qualified as a doctor. That same year, he had to leave his job with Refugee Action and moved to London in order to return to his medical profession and within a year started working as a doctor with the NHS: he is now a GP. Nebi also started and continues to work as a psychotherapist also with the NHS. In 2011, they had their third child, Arian. Baki and Nebi still work and live in London. They have remained close to, and harbour fond memories and respect for, all those who had supported them through their journey towards establishing their lives in the UK. They are proud of the work they do with the NHS and have a great affection for this national institution. They are proud, too, of their three children, who are growing into model citizens and appreciate the UK, the country of their birth, for taking in their parents but are also aware and proud of their Albanian heritage.

Postscript to this account by Baki, whom the author was proud to call her colleague for three years:

The war in the Balkans seemed far away and yet it was close to home. A mere 1,600 miles from London; many had spent summer holidays in Yugoslavia or in nearby Greece. As many of us began to see pictures of fierce fighting on our TV screens in the 1990s there was horrified recognition of places and names. The author's husband watched in disbelief as a Croatian village he had visited on a student holiday trip in 1972 was ripped to bits by airstrikes in front of his eyes. The massacre in Srebrenica unfolded on TV, shaming European governments and leaving ordinary people speechless. It was, as Baki has said, the first genocide in Europe since the Second World War.

The UK government moved slowly, but under Tony Blair's premiership, Paddy Ashdown, the ex-Liberal Democrat leader, was appointed envoy to Kosovo in 1998–9. As an ex-Marine who understood war, but in his own words hated it, he was a good choice. He said that the Serbs had forfeited their rights to rule over Kosovo by their behaviour and in any event they made up only 5 per cent of the population. A targeted bombing campaign was launched against Serbia's capital, Belgrade. Pictures and advocacy aroused great sympathy for the Kosovans.

Chapter 17

The Syrian Crisis

T
he Syrian Civil War, also known as the Syrian uprising or Syrian crisis began on 15 March 2011, with demonstrations against the oppression of the Ba'ath government, whose president is Bashar al-Assad.[1] His family has held the presidency in Syria since 1971. Many of Assad's supporters are Shia while the majority of the government opposition is Sunni, such that politics and religion were inevitably complicated. (Shia and Sunni Islam are the two main branches of the Muslim faith and thus dictate political differences.)

It started during a series of anti-government protests, uprisings and armed rebellions that took place across North Africa and the Middle East in the early 2010s. They began in Tunisia in 2011 in response to poverty and oppression, and, aided by social media, spread rapidly to other countries. A major slogan of the demonstrators in the Arab world is: *ash-sha'b yurīd isqāṭ an-niẓām* (the people want to bring down the regime). The wave of initial revolutions and protests faded by mid-2012, as many Arab Spring demonstrations were met with violent responses from the authorities.

The early hopes that these popular movements would end corruption, increase political participation, and bring about greater economic equality quickly collapsed in the wake of the counter-revolutionary moves by foreign state actors.

In April 2011, the Syrian army fired on demonstrators across the country. After months of military battles, the protests turned into an armed rebellion. Opposition forces were soldiers who had left the Syrian army, and civilian volunteers but the fighters had no central leadership. Battles took place in many towns and cities across the country. In late 2011 various Islamist groups intervened, making a complex situation even more complicated. There had been calls for the US and other Western powers to intervene militarily, especially following allegations that the

Syrian government had used chemical weapons and at a point when it appeared that Bashar's forces were on the brink of defeat. However, at this point with the international community undecided, the Syrian government received military support from Russia as well as from Iran. In many respects, despite the ferocious and destructive war raging, the intervention by Russia was a 'game changer'. The Western forces would now not intervene and risk a war with Russia, who have always seen Syria as an ally and coming within its sphere of influence.

The consequences of Bashar's appalling assault on his own people, aided and abetted by Russia and Iran, have unleashed untold terror, mayhem, destruction and death on the people of Syria, which at the time of writing in 2019 has still not come to an end.

According to the United Nations, by September 2013 over 120,000 people had been killed. In addition, tens of thousands of protesters have been imprisoned and tortured by the Syrian government. International organizations accused both government and opposition forces of breaching human rights. The United Nations said most of the abuses were carried out by the Syrian government.

It was in this context that more than 4 million Syrians were forced to relocate to neighbouring countries, such as Turkey, because of the raging battles.

In the UK, there was a debate about how to respond to this growing international crisis from a humanitarian point of view. The Conservative government under David Cameron's premiership, mindful of a wider domestic debate taking place and with a growing wish to limit the numbers of people coming into the country (whether immigrants, EU nationals or asylum-seekers and refugees), would not make the same commitments as many other countries, such as Canada and Germany had made. It made the case that providing resources for refugee camps in Syria's neighbouring countries would be more effective and welcomed. However, there was still pressure for the government to do more, not least since the media was flooding the country with images of destruction, death and carnage, and the maiming of vulnerable children. The government eventually relented and agreed to evacuate some of the most vulnerable people but from the existing refugee camps, promising to take in up to 20,000 Syrian refugees.

The Office for National Statistics (ONS) produced data between October and December 2017. The figures show that more than 10,000 refugees who fled the crisis in Syria have now been welcomed into the UK through the government's Vulnerable Persons Resettlement Scheme (VPRS).

Refugee Action's analysis revealed that in 2017, 4,832 refugees affected by the conflict in Syria were welcomed into more than 100 local authority areas. This brought the total number of refugees resettled through the government's VPRS to 10,538 people: more than halfway to the pledge to resettle 20,000 by 2020.

The war in Syria has now raged for eight years, longer than the Second World War. The likelihood of peace is unknown since, even if formal hostilities end, those that have fled from their homeland would still be fearful of returning to a country still ruled by Bashar al-Assad or his supporters who have demonstrated such ruthlessness and barbarity in his actions.

The Refugee Integration Scheme in one town: Plymouth

The Refugee Integration Scheme (RIS) is rolled out nationwide.[2] The following is an account of the local scheme in Plymouth which works on a multi -agency basis.

The agencies included are:

Open Doors International Language School (ODILS); Students and Refugees Together (START); Plymouth Access to Housing (PATH); Plymouth City Council; Health; Devon and Cornwall Refugee Support Council (DCRSC); and the Plymouth Race Equality Council.

The health team undertakes the initial assessment, triaging people before they have moved from London. If it is assessed that Plymouth has the appropriate health provision to meet the needs of the families then Plymouth City Council responds to the Home Office and organises for their move to Plymouth.

The team is given health reports from The International Organisation of Migration (IOM) prior to the refugees' arrival so that the team has prior knowledge of a person's physical and mental health issues. Refugees are met within forty-eight hours of arrival and complete a health screening.

The refugees are advised to access a variety of services which have been identified. So far the health team has had no problem meeting the health needs of those sent by the Home Office.

Housing

Under the terms of the nationwide RIS scheme, refugees are only allowed to be placed in private rented housing. By July 2019, 155 individuals and 35 families have had housing arranged for them by local voluntary agencies and charities. These include, as mentioned above, DCRSC, REC, START and PATH.

Language and education

Language classes for both adults and children have been arranged. Adults attend ESOL classes (English as a Second Language) at the Open Doors International Language School (ODILS) and children are accommodated into mainstream education. Young persons aged 16–18 attend the City College and some adults with better English will also attend.

Employment/benefit support

Benefit support is provided by START with some employment support. Those on the scheme with higher levels of English, and who are motivated, have been accepted onto the Positive People programme offered by ODILS for one-to-one mentoring and employment support.

By July 2019, no one was yet in work and many are struggling with learning English. This is an interesting scheme and despite its limited parameters it is providing a supportive service to refugees who have been sent to Plymouth.

Chapter 18

Afterword

T he provision of support for people seeking sanctuary in any receiving country has always been crucial. If men, women and children have been forced to flee from their country of origin with very few possessions or none, then their requirements for safe shelter, food and maintenance and potentially health care will be paramount. The soup kitchens organised for the poor Huguenots and later for the Jews; the food distribution provided for exiles in nineteenth-century London; and the communal meals at Earls Court provided for Belgian refugees, all constituted support for refugees soon after their arrival.

In the latter half of the twentieth century, people seeking sanctuary were able to claim some form of welfare benefits. It was also considered important to assist people of working age progress into work, where appropriate, and therefore be able to contribute to society despite their circumstances.

In this book we have seen that during the 1970s the Ugandan Asians, Chileans and Vietnamese were all able to claim Supplementary Benefit. Whilst this was at 90 per cent of the full rate for UK benefit claimants (and there are reasons for this), nevertheless they were thus helped to become part of the mainstream population and assisted by various agencies to deal with British bureaucracy before they found suitable or even unsuitable employment.

Spurred on by the belief that any foreigners were only arriving into the UK in order to claim benefits, the Conservative government of John Major, 1992–7, began to formulate a policy to remove that support system.

When, at the Conservative party conference in 1992, Peter Lilley vilified people who were in the 'something for nothing society', he included new age travellers, young single mums and 'bogus asylum seekers'. He deliberately struck a note that would resonate with his party members both in the hall and beyond. It paved the way for the 1996 legislation which effectively ended asylum seekers' right to benefits.

Increasingly at that time more people were seeking sanctuary from brutal regimes across the globe. Notably amongst them were Kurds fleeing Saddam Hussein's murderous rule. His policy had been to annihilate them as a group, a genocidal project. The worst of his excesses had been to drop poison gas on the town of Halabja in 1988, killing 5,000 men, women and children. The technique was first to blast house windows from the air so the gas poured directly into people's homes: women and children were thus the most affected. There were ensuing injuries that affected another 12,000 people.

In 1994, the massacre of Tutsis by Hutu peoples in Rwanda killed around a million people. Some refugees sought sanctuary in Britain. Others crossed the border into the Democratic Republic of the Congo. The latter had been in almost constant conflict since independence in 1962 and produced its own refugees, a steady trickle of whom have sought asylum in the UK over the intervening years. Other flash points in the 1990s included Iran, Sierra Leone, Bosnia, and Kosovo.

Since there was now no benefit support, advisors and solicitors had to advocate for their clients through alternative legislation. For single adults the only recourse was through the National Assistance Act 1948. Interestingly we had last seen it used to pay people accommodating Hungarian refugees in 1956–7.

For families with children they argued for support under the Children Act 1989. All of this was much less straightforward than the previous ability to claim Supplementary Benefits and was frequently contested.

Where asylum seekers were living in areas whose councils were not used to such legislation this negotiation could become torturous and people might have to seek out an existence until their case was resolved. This would mean living on handouts from charities, churches and even good neighbours. As many asylum seekers came into the UK via the English Channel crossings into the county of Kent, such as through the port of Dover, Kent County Council ended up supporting both adults and family asylum seekers. With mounting financial pressures they looked to central government to assist.

Under the successor government of Tony Blair, a system was drawn up to support asylum seekers called the National Asylum-Seeking Service (NASS).

To ease pressure on London and the South East, asylum seekers were to be dispersed to centres across the country. They were supposed to stay in that area until their claim was resolved either negatively or positively. The accommodation was stipulated by NASS, unless the person could find a relative to stay with. Provided by private companies, the accommodation was often of poor quality. In each dispersal area there was an agency contracted out by the Home Office to provide asylum advice and support.

Those contracts could be varied and one organisation could lose the ability to provide that advice. Lack of continuity for asylum seekers and staff in organisations could present further problems.

To provide an idea of the scope of the new arrangements there were offices in Birmingham, Nottingham, Derby, Leicester, Leeds, Manchester, Sheffield, Bristol, Plymouth and Portsmouth. There were dedicated offices in both Scotland and Wales. Contracts were also awarded to organisations in relatively smaller dispersal areas

Forms of dispersal had been tried with the Ugandan Asians in 1972–3 and the Vietnamese from 1979 onwards. The dispersal under NASS had a quasi-statutory basis, in that people lost support if they broke the terms of that agreement by moving elsewhere without permission. It could also be breached by misconduct: e.g. damage to property, using drugs on the premises and the like.

It endeavoured to keep people out of London and the South East, although many with friends and relatives there often migrated back, trying to find other non-permitted ways of making a living. For the first time, legislation barred asylum seekers from taking remunerative work. This has long been disputed and the subject of campaigns to remove the restriction. It left the asylum seekers unoccupied and was a major cause of frustration for young active people. It also fed into the myth that they are lazy and don't want to work since the general public has no idea of this restriction. The government left it the tabloid press to present images of asylum seekers and refugees.

Asylum seekers were provided with accommodation. This would be shared for singles, usually but not exclusively for men. Families would be allocated a house or one shared with another family. Asylum 'payment support' was generally two-thirds of income support but it was said that council tax and utilities were paid as part of the accommodation.

In 2015, all support payments, including those for a single parent, adults and children, were levelled down to £36 for each family member per week. In terms of equivalent current prices anyone would be hard pressed to maintain such a weekly budget for food and toiletries. For a single parent this would be doubly hard.

Refugee Action Plymouth

Between 2003 and 2010, the author was the manager for Devon and Cornwall Refugee Action whose office was based in Plymouth. During 2000/2001 Devon County Council had agreed to enter into a contract with the government to support a finite number of asylum seekers from Afghanistan who were housed in Exeter. Whilst there were very small numbers of people across the two counties, the main accommodation was located in Plymouth. This was run by private providers on contracts separate from the one held by Refugee Action. Plymouth had been selected by NASS since accommodation costs were relatively cheaper than those found in the other main cities of Exeter and Truro.

During that time, there were on average 350 asylum seekers accommodated in Plymouth with a maximum of 500. At this point the city's social and economic profile should be referred to.

Plymouth was and is an important naval base which takes pride in its history. The Royal William Yard had been the victualling base for the Royal Navy for centuries. For many years, the city housed the Royal Marines both at Stonehouse Barracks and at the Citadel, which overlooked Plymouth Sound.

Much of the naval fleet assembled to fight during the Falklands War was commanded from Hamoaze House, which is adjacent to the Royal William Yard and had stirred great patriotic fervour in the city.

Just twenty-one years later, in 2003, Britain was engaged in the Iraq war. Whilst among the Iraqi asylum seekers there was support for the aim of ridding the country of Saddam Hussein, many were fearful for their relatives left behind. Many young men in Plymouth saw young Iraqis of military age not returning to fight and 'simply lolling round' the streets with no work. Sometimes this flared up into fights.

The population of Devon and Cornwall in the 1991 census showed people from ethnic groups forming just 0.1 per cent of the population. In many ways it was an area cut off from the rest of the diverse country.

In 1992, Eric Jay wrote a report entitled *Keep them in Birmingham*, challenging racism in south-west England, which reflected both a lack of comprehension and an underlying hostility towards outsiders. By 2000/2001, when asylum seekers started to arrive in Plymouth, these attitudes had changed but only very marginally. They were not helped by articles in the national media pillorying asylum seekers as 'scroungers' in receipt of luxurious accommodation and provided with items such as colour televisions from the government.

Before I paint too bleak a picture, it should be noted that Plymouth Refugee Action was composed of people with many varied talents and the team built had great commitment to doing their very best for their asylum-seeking clients.

As well as the Iraqis, the team was responding to the needs of smaller numbers of Sudanese, Somalians, Congolese, Eritreans and Ethiopians. All the clients had suffered varied degrees of distress and trauma, causing them to flee their home countries, and all needed sensitive handling from the team's caseworkers. They were not involved in the legal immigration work: their job was to ensure the clients' payments from NASS were paid in a timely manner and correctly. If an asylum seeker lost his or her claim he or she was entitled to apply for a Section 4 payment pending possible deportation. These were less than normal payments and might involve being moved, sometimes to another city. Paid by card they were often designated to be cashed at a supermarket 4 or 5 miles from the city centre with no money for bus fares. The caseworkers also liaised over health and education matters.

The team always offered to provide presentations to various agencies to make people aware of the situation facing refugees. From 2006 to 2008 the team received a grant to employ a dedicated refugee awareness worker who designed talks and presentations for schools, community centres and old people's reminiscence groups. Sometimes an asylum seeker or refugee would be happy to accompany the worker to a talk. For example, a young man from Eritrea spoke about his situation prompting an elderly lady to say 'Why that's just like the evacuees who came during the war!'

The team worked locally with both statutory and voluntary agencies. This included social services, health, and, in the early days, the Education Minority Achievement Service. This latter local authority team provided an excellent support service to asylum seekers' children being educated in Plymouth schools. Sadly, the council discontinued it in its original form despite it being very helpful and popular.

The voluntary sector charities working with asylum seekers and refugees were Devon and Cornwall Refugee Support group and for a time Refugees First, both of whom worked mainly with volunteers. START (Students and Refugees Together) used student social workers to support the client group and introduced social work students to the needs of asylum seekers and refugees, whilst at the same time helping those students evidence their understanding of diversity issues as part of their qualification course.

As outlined in Chapter 17, one of the members of this team, Baki Ejupi, became the deputy manager and took the lead in forming Translate Plymouth. This innovative service provided the city with a first-rate translation service for adult refugees and speakers of other languages.

The Plymouth team was part of the national organisation of Refugee Action. The author, as manager, attended regular monthly meetings either in Birmingham or London, discussing contracts, grant applications and projects run by the organisation. The deputy manager and other staff were invited to working groups and all attended Refugee Actions' annual conference.

Unfortunately, in 2010, facing harsh budgetary cuts to the organisation's budget, the Home Office decided to close the Plymouth office, which was a severe blow to both our clients and staff alike. The voluntary agencies of Devon and Cornwall Refugee Council (DCRSC) and the organisation Students, Asylum Seekers and Refugees Together (START) had to take up the slack, an unenviable task since asylum seekers were still being accommodated in Plymouth throughout this period.

Conclusion

We have seen that this country has admitted people fleeing from war and persecution from the sixteenth century onwards. Variously known as Strangers, Huguenots, refugees, exiles, displaced people and asylum seekers they have witnessed varied levels of welcome. That they should feel safe is the first priority. The welcome has been very much predicated on the political situation prevailing here and Britain's view of the country they have fled from. Hence, in the sixteenth and seventeenth centuries Protestant England welcomed people fleeing persecution from Roman Catholic France and Spain. The fact that many had skills such as weaving made them doubly welcome to flagging regional economies. When the Germans invaded Belgium in 1914, the refugees fleeing Britain's enemies were warmly welcomed in this country. During the Cold War those Hungarian refugees who had risen up against the Soviets were, again, warmly welcomed.

It is often said, particularly by policy makers and politicians, that 'we have a proud and welcoming tradition for refugees'. Lucy Mayblin, of Warwick University (2018), has stated that this is a useful phrase for government to use at times of crisis which papers over some of the real issues. We have seen that, during the Nazi era, whilst some Jewish people were admitted the government was ambivalent about working-class Jews. Once the war had started, the policy was to defeat the Nazis at all costs thus obviating the need to rescue Jews and other threatened groups. It was only after the war that governments, horrified at the results of Nazi extermination, decided to unite and establish an international policy framework with the aim of trying to prevent this ever happening again.

However, it should be noted, as Lucy Mayblin evidences, that Britain was a reluctant signatory to the Convention on the status of refugees in 1951, only extending its human rights' clauses to African countries in 1967.

More recent policy and practice to asylum seekers and refugees has seen people dispersed around the country living on very low levels of 'support', not allowed to work in gainful employment and sometimes liable to detention.

This is not to deny the excellent work carried out by national organisations such as Refugee Action and Refugee Council, many local councils, a plethora of church and voluntary organisations involved in support, integration and cultural enhancement for refugees. Churches and mosques have taken an active part in this work and individuals too have given both their time and sometimes accommodation for refugees.

Many people over the centuries have been motivated to welcome and assist, to greater or lesser extent, strangers who have fled circumstances arising in their homelands that they would not wish to experience themselves. It is from such humble acts of humanity that our society becomes enriched.

Notes

Introduction
1. The full text of the Convention can be found at: https://www.unhcr. org/1951-refugee-convention.htm

Chapter 1: The First Protestant Refugees
1. Duke of Alva's execution of the Counts Egmont and Horne. https:// en.wikipedia.org/wiki/Lamoral,_Count_of_Egmont
2. Sourced from Strangers' Hall and Norwich Archives.
3. https://www.britannica.com/event/Massacre-of-Saint-Bartholomews-Day
4. Details taken from London Metropolitan Archives (LMA).
5. Robin Gwynne, *The Huguenots of London*, 2018.
6. Huguenots of Spitalfields. www.huguenotsofspitalfields.org/about-the-huguenots/about-us.html. This is a charity with an extensive website with information about Huguenots across the country.

Chapter 2: The Huguenots and the Revocation of the Edict of Nantes
1. The Huguenot Society of Great Britain and Ireland.
2. Plate showing Royal payments to various French refugees.
3. Huguenots of Spitalfields.
4. C.W. Bracken, *The Huguenot Churches of Plymouth and Stonehouse*, Journals of the Devonshire Association, 1934.
5. Huguenots of Spitalfields.

Chapter 3: The Poor Palatines
1. The Poor Palatines, an 18th-century refugee crisis, British Library. https:// journals.psu.edu/phj/article/download/25606/25375
2. Stoke Newington: Growth, London Road. https://www.british-history. ac.uk/vch/middx/vol8/pp168-171
3. Palatine Heritage Centre at Rathkeale, County Limerick. https://rathkeale. com/palatine-heritage-centre/

Chapter 4: The French Revolution Refugees
1. https://www.geriwalton.com/noyades-drownings-at-nantes/
2. C.W. Bracken, *The Huguenot Churches of Plymouth and Stonehouse*.

3. Record from LMA.
4. Plymouth and West Devon Records Office.* Paper record only.
5. Jean Vidalenc, Louis Blanc: French Politician, https://www.britannica.com/biography/Louis-Blanc
6. https://en.wikipedia.org/wiki/French_Revolution_of_1848
7. https://en.wikipedia.org/wiki/Napoleon_III
8. Panikos Panayi, 'The International Refugee Crisis' in *Refugees in Twentieth-century Britain: A Brief History,* pp 95–112.
9. https://www.historytoday.com/archive/1905-aliens-act

Chapter 5: Portuguese Refugees in Plymouth
1. www.penwithlocalhistorygroup.co.uk/on-this-day/?d=29&id=205
2. Jose Baptista de Sousa, *Holland House and Portugal: English Whiggery and the Constitutional Cause in Iberia.* Anthem Press, 2018.
3. Acland Devon Heritage Centre.

Chapter 6: A Story of Nineteenth- and Twentieth-Century Persecution
1. Helen Fry, *The Jews of Plymouth.*
2. Massacre in the town of Uman by the Haidamacks https://en.wikipedia.org/wiki/Massacre_of_Uman.
3. Rosemary O'Day, *The Jews of London: from Diaspora to Whitechapel.* LSE.
4. David Rosenberg, *Rebel Footprints: A Guide to uncovering London's Radical History.*

Chapter 7: The First World War and Germany invades Belgium
1. https://en.wikipedia.org/wiki/Belgium_in_World_War_I
2. https://flashbak.com/belgian-refugees-in-britain-1914-1918-63285/
3. Imperial War Museum, from Local Government Board.
4. *Common Cause* magazine. London School of Economics (LSE) Women's Library.
5. BBC online recording: History of Belgian refugees at Earls Court. Christophe DeClerq.
6. Women's War Collection, Imperial War Museum.
7. *Common Cause* magazine. LSE Women's Librar.
8. https://www.birminghammail.co.uk/news/nostalgia/birmingham-war-1914-18-coping-refugees-
9. Devon and Cornwall Belgian Refugees Committee; C. Andrew 8/10/1914.
10. www.100firstworldwarstories.co.uk/Louis-Reckelbus/story/
11. From the History Hub. http://historyhub.ie/belgian-refugees-committee-minute-book (Researched by Elizabeth Quin at University College Dublin in 2007).
12. Royal Archives Brussels.
13. Belgian refugees' school. LMA.

14. Devon Heritage Centre. DRP/5.
15. Belgian Village on the Thames, https://www.bvott.org.uk/easttwickenham-st-margarets/

Chapter 8: The Basque Refugee Children
1. https://warwick.ac.uk/services/library/mrc/explorefurther/digital/scw/more/aid/
2. basquechildren.org/-/docs/articles/meirianjumpoxon
3. Don Watson, Politics and Humanitarian Aid. Basque refugees in the North East and Cumbria. https://www.basquechildren.org/-/docs/articles/refugeesnecumbria
4. Aldridge Colony. https://www.basquechildren.org/-/docs/articles/col044
5. www.basquechildren.org/association/research
6. Paige, John *Hearts of Giants*.

Chapter 9: The Nazis and Their Persecution of the Jewish Peoples
1. London, Louise, 'The Aliens Act 1905' in *Whitehall and the Jews 1933–1945*, p.16.
2. London, Louise, 'The Academic Assistance Council' *ibid*, p.47.
3. Council for German Jewry, Minutes of the meeting of the Advisory Committee of the Refugee Organisations to the High Commissioner for Refugees from Germany – 2793 01 02 03–04, Woburn House 15 June 1936.
4. London, Louise, *Whitehall and the Jews*, p.35.
5. Fund for German Jewry 1936. LMA ACC 2793 01 01 01.
6. The government's Cabinet Committee on Aliens Restriction first met with the British Board of Deputies to negotiate various matters on 6 April 1933. Louise, London, p27.
7. London, Louise, 'Polish Jews trapped at the border', *Whitehall and the Jews*, p.97.
8. London Louise, 'Robert Stopford, Mission in Czechoslovakia' ibid, p.146.
9. Kindertransport Association. Info@kindertransport.org.
10. Refugees Llantryd Wells, BBC November 2018.

Chapter 10: Second World War Refugees in Britain
1. https://www.pressandjournal.co.uk/fp/news/moray/buckie/1689481/the-wartime-refugees-who-gave-buckie-then-nickname-little-norway/
2. https://www.independent.co.uk/news/people/obituary-professor-ralph-miliband-1438110.html
3. Lucy Masterman Papers.
4. Dartington papers at Devon Heritage Centre. DWE.
5. Louise, London, 'Francis Meynell' in *Whitehall and the Jews*, p.208.
6. Louise, London, 'Archbishop of Canterbury', *ibid*, p.209.

7. https://www.telegraph.co.uk/history/world-war-two/11370972/Holocaust-Memorial-Day-Telegraph-revealed-Nazi-gas-chambers-three-years-before-liberation-of-Auschwitz.html
8. Louise, London, 'The British response to the Holocaust up to the end of 1942' in *Whitehall and the Jews*, p.197.

Chapter 11: The Displacement of Peoples after the Second World War

1. https://en.m.wikipedia.org/wiki/Displaced_persons_camps_in_post-World_War_II_Europe
2. European refugees after 1945. Coming to Britain. University of Nottingham 2012.
3. https://changingidentities.wordpress.com/
4. Who were the Windrush Poles? www.britishfuture.org/articles/windrush-poles/
5. Agata Blaszczyk, The resettlement of Polish refugees after the Second World War, https://www.fmreview.org/resettlement/blaszczyk
6. The Lake District Holocaust Project.

Chapter 12: The Hungarian Uprising

1. The Hungarian Revolution of 1956. https://en.wikipedia.org/wiki/Hungarian_Revolution_of_1956
2. Hungarian Refugees. MCC/CH/CD/01/0181 (LMA).
3. Photo of Hungarian Refugees at Astor Hall. Will be available in spring 2020 at Plymouth's new museum *The Box*.
4. Hungarian Refugee Students 1956–1958. ED 121/874 The National Archives.
5. Escape from Hungary by Tom Leimdorfer, BBC website. October 2006.

Chapter 13: The Ugandan Asians

1. https://en.wikipedia.org/wiki/Expulsion_of_Asians_from_Uganda
2. Ugandan Asian Resettlement Board.
3. Taylor, Becky, *Good Citizens? Ugandan Asians, Volunteers and 'Race' Relations in 1970s Britain*. https://ueaeprints.uea.ac.uk/65522/1/Published_manuscript.pdf
4. https://libcom.org/tags/imperial-typewriters-strike
5. https://www.theguardian.com/uk/2002/aug/11/race.world
6. https://hansard.parliament.uk/Lords/2012-12 06/debates/12120659000796/UgandanAsians

Chapter 14: The Chilean Coup and its Aftermath

1. Disputed admission of 7 Chileans. The National Archives 1974. HO 394/260.
2. Proposed total number refugees to be accepted by UK 1974–1977. The National Archives HO 394/277 277.

3. https://api.parliament.uk/historic-hansard/commons/1973/dec/20/chilean-refugees#S5CV0866P0_19731220_HOC_194

4. Voluntary services unit would be responsible to assist with grants for resettlement of Chilean refugees. The National Archives HO 376/196

5. Briefing paper from the National Museum of Labour History which holds the archive of the Chile Solidarity Campaign.

6. Records of Birmingham Chile Solidarity Campaign. https://warwick.ac.uk/services/library/mrc/explorefurther/images/chile/local/

7. https://en.wikipedia.org/wiki/Nae_Pasaran. Film is also available on BBC I player.

Chapter 15: A Vietnamese Story

1. Viet Ventures, a brief history of Vietnam. www.vietventures.com/Vietnam/history_vietnam.asp

2. British Government discussions on resettlement June 1979. The National Archives HO 376/201.

3. Greater London Council policy on rehousing. LMA DG/TD/1/25.

4. *The Vietnamese Community in Great Britain, Thirty Years on.* The Runneymede Trust.

5. Meiklejohn, Julia, *Early Work with Refugees (Save the Children & Refugee Action): A narrative account.* August 2018.

Chapter 16: The Balkan Wars in the 1990s and the Kosovo Humanitarian Evacuation Programme

1. Dr Baki Ejupi, *Background to War in the Balkans.* Summer 2019.

2. Dr Baki Ejupi, *Having to leave Kosovo and a new life in the UK.* Personal account.

Chapter 17: The Syrian Crisis

1. www.iamsyria.org/conflict-background.html provided background to the war and to refugees leaving Syria.

2. Account of local Plymouth operation of Refugee Integration Scheme.

Bibliography

British Refugee Council, *Asylum-seekers in the United Kingdom* (1989).

Burn, John Southerden, *The history of the French, Walloon, Dutch and other foreign Protestant refugees settled in England 1798–1870 (1846)*.

Cahalan, P., *Belgian Refugee Relief in England during the Great War* (1982).

Chater, Kathy, *Tracing Your Huguenot Ancestors* (2015).

Dalglish, C., *Refugees from Vietnam* (1989).

Endelman, Todd M., *The Jews of Britain: 1656 to 2000* (2002).

Glenny, Misha, *The Balkans* (2017).

Gwynn, Robin, *The Huguenots of London* (2018).

Gwynn, Robin, *Huguenot Heritage: the History and Contribution of the Huguenots in Britain* (1985).

Hokayem, Emile, *Syria's Uprising and the Fracturing of the Levant* (2013).

Holmes, C., 'Immigrants, Refugees and Revolutionaries', in Slatter, J. (ed.), *From the Other Shore: Russian Political Immigrants in Britain, 1880–1917* (1984).

Kuepper, W. G., Lackey, G. L. and Swinnerton, E. M., *Ugandan Asians in Great Britain* (1975).

Legarreta, D., *The Guernica Generation: Basque Refugee Children of the Spanish Civil War* (1984).

London, Louise, *Whitehall and the Jews 1933–1948: British Immigration Policy and the Holocaust* (2000).

London, Louise, 'Jewish Refugees, Anglo Jewry and British Government Policy, 1930–1940', in D. Cesarani (ed.), *The Making of Modern Anglo-Jewry* (1990).

Parris, S.J., *Sacrilege* (2012).

Porter, B., *The Refugee Question in Mid-Victorian Politics* (1979).

Rosenberg, David, *Rebel Footprints: A Guide to uncovering London's Radical History* (2015).

de Sousa, Jose Baptista, *Holland House and Portugal: English Whiggery and the Constitutional Cause in Iberia* (2018).

Sansom, C. J., *Winter in Madrid* (2006).

Simmons, John, *Spanish Crossings* (2018).

Index

VILLA GRINALDI 140